AMERICAN CHILDHOODS

A Series Edited by James Marten

Children of the Western Plains

Children of the Western Plains

The Nineteenth-Century Experience

MARILYN IRVIN HOLT

Ivan R. Dee

CHICAGO 2003

Library of Congress Cataloging-in-Publication Data:
Holt, Marilyn Irvin, 1949–
    Children of the western plains : the nineteenth-century experience /
    Marilyn Irvin Holt.
        p. cm. — (American childhoods)
    Includes bibliographical references and index.
    ISBN 1-56663-540-3
        1. Pioneer children—Great Plains—History—19th century. 2. Immigrant children—Great Plains—History—19th century. 3. Children—Great Plains—History—19th century. 4. Frontier and pioneer life—Great Plains. 5. Great Plains—Social life and customs—19th century. 6. Great Plains—Social conditions—19th century. 7. Pioneer children—Great Plains—Biography. 8. Immigrant children—Great Plains—Biography. 9. Children—Great Plains—Biography. I. Title. II. Series.

F596.H6835 2003
978'.02'083—dc21   2003046050

To my husband, Daniel, a Kansas kid

Contents

Children of the Western Plains

Introduction

ON DECEMBER 7, 1828, Lewis Bissell Dougherty was born at Cantonment Leavenworth, the Missouri River post that later became Fort Leavenworth. As an adult, Dougherty was a successful banker and civic leader, but there was a footnote attached to his name. He was one of the first white children born in Kansas. State, local, and family histories have found it important, even mandatory, to list "firsts"—the first homesteaders in an area, first schoolhouse, first church. It should be no surprise, then, that first births among Euro-Americans were recorded as noteworthy events. The children were symbolic of the thousands that followed, either as "native-born" Westerners or migrants to the Great Plains. Youngsters like Dougherty were only the initial wave of children that would look back on their growing-up years and express sentiments similar to that proclaimed by a Kansas resident early in the twentieth century: "As for me I feel that I grew up with the country."[1]

With westward expansion and settlement, children filled the ranks of Great Plains settlers, military and missionary dependents. Some were recorded for posterity, but virtually nothing was said or written about most of them. Details about the lives of Western families have been left to the imagination and popular notions. Until very recently, historians of Western life overlooked children as active participants with their own perceptions, roles, and experiences. Children appear as a supporting cast, without a great deal to do but worry parents or provide an amusing vignette. In Merrill Mattes's ground-breaking *The Great Platte River Road,* for example, child travelers are secondary to the story of men and women on the trail; in publications dealing with women in the West, children are considered within the context of women's responsibilities.

Having said that, there is a small but expanding collection of literature that focuses in one way or another on youngsters and childhood in the American West. Among these are Emmy E. Werner's *Pioneer Children on the Journey West* and Susan Arrington Madsen's *I Walked to Zion;* both are accounts of overland migration. *Settlers' Children* by Elizabeth Hampsten is primarily concerned with youngsters in the Dakotas; Cathy Luchetti presents an overview of frontier families in *Children of the West;* and Patricia Y. Stallard studies military dependents in *Glittering Misery.* Some of these books are more anecdotal than interpretive, and most appeared after Elliott West's analytical and thought-provoking *Growing Up with the Country,* with its focus on Euro-American families in the overland migrations, in Rocky Mountain mining districts, and on early farms or ranches on the plains or in the American Southwest.[2]

In this book, my scope encompasses Euro-Americans who migrated to the plains from within the United States; immigrants who came directly from Europe; and African Americans who arrived after the Civil War. It is a cross section of homesteaders, town builders, missionaries, and military dependents. Since other publications have treated the subject of white homesteaders, there is no need to reexamine *only* that segment of the population. It is important, on the other hand, to consider the immigrant presence since it made up a majority in some areas at specific times; in Nebraska, as one example, 54 percent of the population in 1870 represented foreign-born adults and children.[3]

This is not intended as a comparative study between the immigrant or African-American experience and that of American-born whites, and it does not include other plains residents such as Native American children, the Chinese who could be found in mining and railroad towns, or native-born Hispanics or Mexican migrants. Nevertheless the inclusion of diverse European immigrant groups and of African-American settlers is meant to recognize the diversity of plains residents and explore shared or disparate perceptions and experiences. It is worth considering whether the Great Plains experience transcended diverse religious, ethnic, and racial backgrounds to produce a perception of regional identity.

Children are defined as anyone under sixteen, fully realizing that different stages of maturity produce quite different perspectives. The age limit is arbitrary, but it seems reasonable to exclude older teens whose roles and expectations were those of young adults. "I am now eighteen years of age, and must begin to assume life's responsibilities, and not shrink from unpleasant and untried realities," wrote Mollie Dorsey in 1857 as she, her parents, and seven younger siblings prepared to move to Nebraska.[4] As a spokesperson for her family, Mollie does appear, however, in the narrative. So too do many youngsters who recorded their lives in diaries and letters or as adults penned reminiscences and published accounts. The reader will find the voices of some threaded throughout the text because they had a great deal to say about a great many things.

Children's experiences are examined in the broad categories of expectations and perceptions, settlement, work and play, education, community and family life, and mortality. These are considered against a backdrop of Western expansionism, regional identity, assimilation, and American society's cultural standards for what constituted proper childrearing practices and typified a wholesome, healthy childhood. Settlement and town building did not occur in an environment devoid of cultural or social dictates. People brought their traditions and customs to the plains, and to a great extent they attempted to replicate the familiar in a new environment. Their intellectual and cultural baggage included ideas about children and childhood. How easily the Western environment allowed adult perceptions to persist, or influenced change, is evaluated in terms of children's behavior and viewpoint.

The geographical region for this book was limited to the American Great Plains, which is divided into the Northern, Central, Southern, and High Plains. The entire region ends where the Rocky Mountains begin, but where its eastern boundary begins is more difficult to decide. In 1868 geologist and explorer John Wesley Powell placed the eastern boundary at the 100th meridian, placing the following within the Great Plains: eastern Montana, Wyoming, Colorado, and New Mexico; western North Dakota, South Dakota, Nebraska, Kansas, and Oklahoma; part of western Texas and all of the Texas Panhandle. Today the eastern line is more commonly accepted as the 98th meridian, farther east, although that too remains a point of discussion. Some nongeographers have disregarded physical determinants such as rainfall amounts, presence of shortgrass and tallgrass prairies, and soil types. They have defined the Great Plains in terms of cultural attitudes and regional behavior. In doing so, these observers of plains life have liberally pushed back the line to include all but the most eastern edges of Kansas, Nebraska, the Dakotas, and Oklahoma. They have taken the approach suggested by the historian Paula Nelson: "Exact boundaries may not be important. . . . You will know you are there when you arrive."[5] I have pushed the boundary as far east as possible, especially for Kansas and Nebraska in their pre-territorial periods. The reason is simple. Euro-American children in these areas arrived early, living on what was the very edge of America's nineteenth-century frontier. In the early 1800s they had barely reached the 95th meridian, let alone the 98th. If they were not by geographical definition on the Great Plains, they were certainly at the front door.

Generally the century of plains settlement can be divided into three stages: the pre-territorial period, when a few Euro-American families were attached to a small number of Western forts and Indian missions; the territorial period, which opened up specific areas for settlement; and statehood, when the majority of homesteaders and town builders arrived on the plains. Within the region of the Great Plains, localized land booms periodically attracted large numbers of settlers, and economic downturns and natural calamities forced times of flight. The population was mobile, and youngsters were likely to live in more than one place. Settlement was not a steady wave or progression, and frontier conditions did not simply cease to exist at the end of the nineteenth century. If youngsters growing up in Nebraska during the 1870s could have stepped forward in time to Montana during the 1890s, they would have found that not much had changed. And, into the twentieth century, many children had the same experiences as those of an earlier generation. Eight-year-old Enid Bern was thrilled with the prospect of homesteading in North Dakota: "It was May 1, 1907, when we stepped off the train. Organized Hettinger County was fourteen days old." In 1910 the family of six-year-old Josephine Boltz moved into a two-room sod house in western Kansas; the family's Missouri relatives "thought we were leaving civilization forever."[6]

Although frontier conditions persisted well into the 1900s in some places, this book does not pursue children's experiences into the twentieth century. It focuses on children of the 1800s and explores their lives in terms of what they saw, heard, believed, and lived. Children were viable, necessary contributors to the settlement process. They were the reason for building schools and organizing Sunday schools, and they were at the center of adult concerns and delights. By the end of the century they were the objects of study and discussion for professionals in social welfare, education, and medicine. The attention given children, as well as their own sense of involvement, are examined and explored to discover common themes in children's lives and the experiences of a Western childhood.

CHAPTER ONE

Perceptions and Expectations

———————

IN EARLY MARCH 1876 a group of Swedish settlers left Illinois for south central Nebraska, where snow blew across open land littered with "hundreds of thousands of bleaching buffalo skeletons." Just days after the homesteaders reached their destination, a boy was born to the Nelson family. Wrote a nineteen-year-old diarist in the group: "Charley Nelson's already large family was further increased by the arrival today of a little 'bug eater.' . . . He was born in Shafer's house and is the first child of Swede descent born in Phelps County." In a strange environment, something very normal had occurred, and time after time those new to the plains recorded the first child born to a family in a homesteading party or to someone in a nearby community. It was an affirmation that life went on, no matter the unfamiliar landscape or obstacles that lay ahead.[1]

Children of homesteaders and town builders were not, however, the first Euro-American children in the West. Long before the little "bug eater," Atle Nelson, entered the world in 1876, the plains saw the offspring of military personnel, federal employees and contractors, fur traders, and missionaries. Lucia Francis Pixley, the daughter of missionaries working among the Osage Indians in the 1820s, was "the *first white child*" [original emphasis] born in present-day Kansas; the second to be born in Kansas was Napoleon Boone, the son of Daniel M. Boone, an "agriculturist" employed by the government for the Kansa Indians; and the third child, Lewis Bissell Dougherty, born in 1828, was the son of an Indian agent.[2]

Before the mid-1840s and the first major migration west of the Mississippi, some families lived beyond the states and territories that were considered at the time to be the Western frontier. When commentators noticed them, it was usually to describe the female response to conditions. The consensus was that the woman "is terribly scared . . . and with what interest she inquires about . . . fevers and Indians." Although the description was meant to point out female weaknesses, any cautious person, male or female, would have expressed concerns. Marginal diets, poor sanitation, and negligible ventilation in dwellings brought on debilitating and potentially deadly maladies. Smallpox, typhoid, tuberculosis, cholera, and pneumonia stalked the Westerner. If disease did not kill, there was the possibility that Indians fighting against white encroachment would. Threats of hostilities routinely raised alarms. Western life was precarious and unpredictable. Nevertheless Euro-American families pushed the frontier by moving onto the plains during the first decades of the nineteenth century.[3]

How many children experienced life on the plains during the early 1800s can only be guessed. The picture is clouded by the popular notion that the region was known to only a few Euro-Americans—mountain men and fur traders, priests, explorers, and military men. Certainly the federal government had little, if any, idea of employees' domestic arrangements or the number of civilian dependents on army posts. (Accurate counts for post residents were not required until 1891.) It was much the same for missionaries, whose reports emphasized successes and failures in winning Indian converts. Only occasionally were missionaries' children mentioned in correspondence and official reports. From the latter we know, for example, that Moses and Sarah Pearson arrived at Shawnee Friends Mission (Kansas) with five children in 1837. The oldest, Rhoda, was twelve; the youngest, Joshua, was three. Seven years later, James and

Caroline Wheeler began mission work among the Wyandot Indians. With them were three children—John, Thomas, and Mary. What we do not know with any certainty is how many other children were Western residents.[4]

The child population of the West may have been small, but presence of children dispels the notion that the region was a man's world. In fact, meticulous compilations made by Louise Barry for pre-territorial Kansas contain references to children that, in turn, provide some idea of births in that region. From this a clearer view emerges. Between 1800 and 1854, forty-seven Euro-American children were born in the area now known as Kansas. Only one child, Susannah Yoacham, was born to a family with no direct link to government, military, or missionary employment; the family, evidently related to an Indian agent, stayed only briefly in Kansas. Of the remaining births in pre-territorial Kansas, four were children of military families; two of these, Louisa and George (who died at ten months), were the children of Col. Stephen W. and Mary Kearny at Fort Leavenworth. Six were born to government employees or contractors, but the largest number, thirty-six, were children of missionaries. In addition to those born on this Western frontier, there were older brothers and sisters who traveled to the area with their parents. Annie Elizabeth Dougherty, as one example, accompanied her parents to Cantonment Leavenworth and was about four years old when her brother Lewis Bissell was born there.[5]

The first Euro-Americans living on the Great Plains did not think of childhood in the same way as farmers and town builders did at the end of the 1800s. This is not to say that early nineteenth-century parents loved their children less or disregarded the idea of childhood. Rather, it is an expression of attitudes that changed over a century. In the early 1800s many Americans continued to accept the Puritan tenet that children were by nature the inheritors of original sin. Childhood was viewed as a relatively short stage which ended at about age six. In this context, parents could show no greater love for their children than suppressing a child's inborn wickedness. These beliefs were being challenged, however, by philosophers and educators, notably Jean-Jacques Rousseau, who argued that children came into the world as innocents. Adults need not worry about repressing their innate evil of original sin. Rather, they should carefully guide children through developmental phases that extended the time of childhood. This line of thinking coexisted with Puritan thought, but gradually the emphasis on child innocence gained acceptance. The idea began to appear more frequently in childrearing literature of the 1830s. By the 1850s it became the norm.

Among the more influential authors in the emerging genre of child-care publications was Lydia Child. A writer and reformer, Child confidently announced in *The Mother's Book* (1831) that children "come to us from heaven, with their little souls full of innocence and peace." Mothers faced the momentous challenge of protecting children while preparing them for a less-than-innocent world. Mrs. Child was an opinionated taskmaster, warning against stories and fables that had no "clear and simple moral" and parties that allowed youngsters to eat sweets and "dress in finery." During the remainder of the century, a chorus of advisers emerged as the number of publications interested in childhood steadily increased. *Godey's Magazine and Lady's Book, Monthly Religious Magazine,* and *The Mother's Assistant and Young Lady's Friend* were among the journals that consistently discussed child development and home education. The dissemination of ideas and practical information, as well as romanticized portrayals of children, created an image of children and told a largely middle-class readership what constituted an ideal childhood.[6]

One might expect that women living on the military and missionary frontier were untouched by early nineteenth-century debates over the nature of children, that they were unaware of childrearing advice offered through the printed page. Books, after all, were a luxury, and publications from the East were slow to arrive. Nevertheless these women were a potential audience. By the standards of the times, officers' wives were well educated and attuned to social expectations. Missionary women could read and write, and their work put them in contact with religious thought on the subject of child nature. Although isolated, these women were, as a rule, from a middle class that was literate and conscious of public discourse, society's view of children, and the probability of being harshly judged if they failed to follow social standards.

Women as well as men went about rearing children under demanding circumstances. Cantonment Leavenworth, established in 1827 and renamed Fort Leavenworth in 1832, was described as a collection of "miserable huts." Elizabeth Custer, writing of Fort Lincoln in Dakota Territory, recalled cramped housing "put together with as few materials as possible." "In one set of quarters," she wrote, "there chanced to be so many children and so little room that the parents had invented a three-story bed, where the little ones could be all stowed at night." At Camp Cooke, Montana Territory, roofs leaked when it rained, and "Mrs. N[ugent] found her three months old baby lying in its crib with muddy water dripping in its face." Writing of his trip up the Missouri River to Cantonment Leavenworth in 1829, Second Lt. Philip St. George Cooke was surprised to find soldiers sharing space with women and children. "[It] was remarkable how large the proportion of married men were among those selected to fill our companies. . . . The boat swarmed with their wives and children; the deck was barricaded with beds and bedding; infants squalled . . . and in the guise of the founders of a colony, we *set forth* [original emphasis] for our adventures."[7]

These "founders of a colony" fluctuated in number. Military personnel were usually on temporary duty, awaiting the next set of orders. Philip St. George Cooke's assignments were clear testimonials to the moves faced by army families. One Cooke daughter was born in Indian Territory (present-day Oklahoma) in 1840; another daughter came along two years later when Cooke was reassigned to Leavenworth. Rachel Lobach, born at Carlisle, Pennsylvania, in 1858, moved to Fort McPherson (Nebraska) in 1865 with her sister, mother, and stepfather. After six months at McPherson, they went to Fort Omaha for a year. Then it was on to Fort Sanders (Wyoming) before going to Medicine Bow, Wyoming Territory, where her stepfather was part of the army contingent protecting Union Pacific construction workers. In two years Rachel moved four times, and in each place she encountered other youngsters like herself, including a girl at Medicine Bow whose father was a railroad section boss. Military dependents learned early to adapt. They might remember one place more fondly than another, but they understood that army life was one of change. Mary Leefe lived on six military posts west of the Missouri River by the time she was sixteen. "Always on entering a fort," she wrote, "we children picked out the best and the worst, but more usually the best spots."[8]

Children were among the transients in a frontier society. Any number, not all of them military dependents, spent a part or all of their growing-up years on the move. The older of two "sunbrowned" girls encountered by Horace Greeley on his westward trek in 1859 was only ten years old, but already she had traveled from Missouri to Wyoming to a makeshift stagecoach stop in Kansas. A young Anne Ellis traversed the plains three times, and Marian Sloan Russell made five round-trip crossings of the Santa Fe Trail between the ages of seven and seventeen. "Mother," she wrote, "was never quite happy unless she were passing back and forth over it . . . or planning to."[9]

Whether on the move or stopped, children received attention from adults who worried about their welfare and attempted to replicate experiences associated with "civilization." Daniel M. Boone sent at least six of his twelve children to school at the short-lived Kansa Methodist Mission. They studied side-by-side with Indian youngsters, as did the three daughters of the Reverend Watt A.

Duncan, who in the 1870s worked among the Cherokees in Indian Territory. At Fort Lincoln, clothing rather than schooling posed a specific need, and Elizabeth Custer, with other ladies of the garrison, rallied to make "suitable" attire for a family of children. Catharine Hertzog, living with her daughter and son-in-law at Cantonment Leavenworth, worried about the material things her grandchildren did not have. In letters to relatives in Philadelphia, she asked that they send "two necklaces for Marys [*sic*] children" and "original poems and another amusing book for a child learning to read."[10]

Lure of the Plains

Until the 1850s, Euro-Americans were a distinct minority on the plains. The region was inhabited by a richly diverse number of Native American tribes with their own cultural practices, economic structures, and languages. For some, the plains were traditional homeland, but others were recent arrivals, having been pressured to leave eastern sections of the United States for reserves in the West. The newly relocated often reacted to the plains environment in much the same way as Euro-Americans. "We had always lived in the timber and did not like the Prairie," said a Cherokee girl whose family left Tennessee for Indian Territory. Forced removal to the West and conflicts on the plains reflected the torturous history of Indian-white relations that rested on federal promises of land in perpetuity and the American appetite for expansion. With Euro-American advancement, the federal government declared more and more Indian lands part of the public domain. This in turn opened the way for settlement and subsequent creation of territories and then states. In this battle for land, Oklahoma remained an Indian territory until 1889 when a portion opened for white settlement. (Another section, the Cherokee Outlet, commonly called the

In Custer County, Nebraska, a family pauses on the way to a new home-stead. *(Solomon D. Butcher Collection, Nebraska State Historical Society)*

Cherokee Strip, opened in 1893 and paved the way for Oklahoma statehood in the early twentieth century.) Although a large population of various Indian groups occupied Oklahoma during the 1800s, white America considered it wild and unsettled because Caucasians had not established the towns, farms, or social institutions that existed there. Clara Ewell clearly accepted this idea when she wrote of her family's move from Iowa. They were going to the "unsettled territory" of the Cherokee Strip.[11]

Of course, when migration began in earnest in the late 1840s, few emigrants, entrepreneurs, or adventurers looking for the West stopped on the plains. One forty-niner, unimpressed with the Platte River Valley, wrote: "If the Government would offer me a patent of all the land from Fort Kearny to Fort Laramie I would not accept it." California gold lured him and thousands more. Oregon country beckoned others with the promise of cheap land. The plains remained a place to hurry through rather than a place to stay. Labeled the "Great American Desert" after Maj. Stephen H. Long's 1819–1820 expedition, the region conjured up images of a vast wasteland unfit for agriculture. One explorer predicted that the plains would become "as celebrated as the sandy deserts of Africa," and Gen. William T. Sherman is said to have declared, "If I owned both hell and Texas, I'd rent out Texas and live in hell."[12]

The plains presented problems that tended to alarm rather than entice. Rivers were not always the predictable, navigable waterways so familiar to Eastern residents. One traveler described the Platte as "too thin to walk on, too thick to drink, too shallow for navigation . . . the most disappointing and least useful stream in America."[13] Depth and consistency of flow made travel and transport of goods difficult on more than one Western river. Much of the terrain—sandhills, treeless buttes, open grassland—bore little resemblance to the landscapes known to those living east of the Missouri River. Broad variations in climate, rainfall, and soil quality were not fully understood until settlement in the 1870s rapidly filled the eastern plains and forced would-be settlers beyond the 98th meridian to a semi-arid environment. Water was critical. In many places it was almost nonexistent or of poor quality. Weather conditions fluctuated from searing heat to frigid winters and included blizzards, drought, tornadoes, hail, dust, and wind. And there was the look of the plains, which prompted many to keep moving west or turn back east. Wide spaces without timber promised to be physically demanding and psychologically intimidating.

Given its reputation as uninhabitable and its inherent challenges, one has to wonder why anyone ventured onto the plains with the intention of staying. Certainly those connected with the military, with government programs for native groups, and missionaries had defined reasons for being there. But what of those who came as settlers and town builders? What possible motivations, hopes, dreams, even lunacy prompted people to halt their westward trek in the center of the nation?

Part of the answer can be found in public opinion. By mid-century, Americans were emboldened by overland migration to Oregon and California as well as emigration into Texas. American society was consumed with the call of Manifest Destiny. People began to believe that there were no limits to America as one frontier after another was overcome. Self-confidence was helped along by an expanding military presence that offered protection. Just as important, people were attracted to the plains by booster rhetoric and scientific claims that the Great American Desert could be transformed into a paradise because "rain followed the plow." The prairie, so the theory said, would lose its "water-shedding roof" once the plow turned up the ground. Land cultivation and planted trees increased humidity and attracted rain like a magnet. "Scientific" reports promised that moisture and rainfall were natural results of settlement. Whether potential settlers were tricked by such claims or allowed themselves to be deluded by them made little difference. They came. And when their arrival coincided with periods of abundant rainfall, the promises of a Garden of Eden seemed true.[14]

The plains soon began to attract families disillusioned with one place and willing to move on. Joshua Wheatcroft's family was a good example of the inclination to see if life and luck were better on the plains. Joshua's parents left England, settled in Pennsylvania, and then moved to Iowa. In 1880 the family packed up and moved one more time, settling in western Kansas. In the same year Hamlin Garland's family decided to relocate—once again. In his *A Son of the Middle Border*, Garland recalled his "carefree" school life in Iowa, but the farm economy, besieged by poor crops and grasshoppers, was faltering. "My father," wrote Garland, "turned his face toward the free lands of the farther west. He became again the pioneer. DAKOTA was the magic word."[15]

By the mid-1800s the plains attracted speculators, town builders, and homesteaders. When the Kansas-Nebraska Act of 1854 opened Kansas and Nebraska territories for settlement, and the Dakota Territory was organized in 1861, the preemption law of 1841 allowed settlers to select 160 acres from the public domain with first option to buy at $1.25 per acre when the government offered land for sale. By the end of the 1850s the Pikes Peak gold rush brought prospectors and their families to what became Colorado; and later, gold beckoned from the Black Hills of the Dakotas. Another type of prospector came too. This was the town speculator who took advantage of the Townsite Preemption Act of 1844 (amended in 1867) to purchase land and plat it into town lots for sale. After the Civil War the plains began to fill with immigrants from Europe, ex-slaves from Southern states, and war veterans who went home to Illinois or Ohio or New York, packed up the wife and kids, and headed west to take advantage of land laws that promised ownership.

The Homestead Act (1862) specified 160 acres for anyone who was head of household or 21 years old and who was a United States citizen or declared his or her intention to become one. (The act did not discriminate against women.) To receive ownership, the homesteader was required to pay a $10 filing fee, live on the land for 5 years, and "improve" it with a built structure and cultivated land. The Timber Culture Act (1873) provided 160 acres to anyone who planted 40 acres in trees and maintained them for 10 years; in 1878 the number was modified to a more realistic ten acres. The Desert Land Act (1877) promised a full section of land, at $1.25 per acre, if the land was placed under irrigation. Finally, land could be purchased from railroads that sold property granted to them by the federal government but not used to complete routes. Settlers could choose more than one of these options, and during the century's last three decades, new arrivals purchased homesteads relinquished by settlers who were ready to leave.

Federal land laws offered attractive inducements to Europeans as well as Americans. From Russia's agricultural regions to Scandinavia to Ireland, people faced political and social unrest, suppression of religious beliefs, and famine. There were innumerable reasons to consider immigration. Within the United States there were problems too. Periodically national depressions actually encouraged western migration. The Panic of 1857, for example, prompted families to try to recoup their losses in the new territories. Depressions in 1873, 1887, and 1893 had the same effect, while also forcing many already on the plains to seek another place to start over. The rising cost of land in Eastern states was an additional factor. If a family longed to own land rather than rent, homesteading was a viable option. For many, the lure of the West was its potential for speculative schemes, whether in gold, town building, or cattle. White backlash to Reconstruction in the South created another kind of incentive to migrate. African Americans, freed from slavery but living in a climate of poverty and persecution, turned to the North or West for something better. No matter their place of origin or diversity of backgrounds, potential Westerners shared in a hope, if not a firm belief, that the West offered infinite possibilities for personal success and prosperity.

The age and gender of children, as well as parental tendencies to share information, shaped youngsters' understanding of the decision to migrate. With no evidence to the contrary, Dakota-bound James Walker chalked up the move to his parents catching "western fever." Any number, however, understood that economics played a key role. One girl knew that her extended family was drawn to Kansas by "glowing tales of the opportunities there . . . for free land," and a teenage boy, thinking of "hard up" neighbors and friends back in Illinois, decided that after one year of Kansas homesteading his family had "done well considering the means we had." Mollie Dorsey, destined for Nebraska, was circumspect. Her father "met with reverses," making it difficult to support a family of eight children in Indiana. When relatives urged the Dorseys to join them in Nebraska Territory, it was an "alluring" inducement. Throughout the century the West was characterized as a place that allowed individuals to escape old problems and begin over. The Dorsey family looked for something better in 1857 when a national depression threatened the family's economic stability. The Siceloff family, which lost its farm during the financial panic of 1893, hoped to start

African Americans served on the military frontier, established home-steads, or, like this young family, lived in towns. *(Kansas State Historical Society)*

over and succeed in Oklahoma. Said eight-year-old David, "the set-tlement of the Cherokee Strip was our chance to get on our feet again."[16]

For Grace Russell's family, economics was a consideration, but to her mind the move from Pennsylvania coal mining to Kansas homesteading was about personal freedom. Her father wanted to be his own boss. Her mother wanted the children to grow up where they were anyone's equal and would never be called "coal miner's brats." The West was not only a place that allowed people to start over, it released them from derogatory stereotypes and oppressive social rankings. It was idealized as a place where status, class, and family name mattered little. Individuals were judged on personal merits. "Family name," wrote one Westerner, "cuts but little figure. It's the character of the man that wins recognition."

Improving one's economic standing was admired, if not expected, but poverty was not necessarily a stigma or sign of in-dolence. To condemn someone for being poor was, after all, tanta-mount to dismissing a large portion of the population. In the absence of money and material goods as a measure of a person's worth, character became a larger issue. African-American settlers, with little money and few farm implements, faced racism, but they also received nodding approval from white neighbors because "[they] know how to work, and are not afraid to do it." David Siceloff recalled impoverished neighbors in Oklahoma. The four boys wore "faded and patched waists and pants," and the two girls had nothing to wear but flour sacks "with neck and arm holes." Despite their poverty, they were not stigmatized. In fact the family was well liked because everyone worked, was well behaved, and "we never heard profanity or vulgar language from any of them."[17]

In the imagined West, rugged individualism was rewarded in an egalitarian society. Its rural character was romanticized as the place where the national identity with agrarian traditions remained intact. As the United States experienced a rise in population and urbanization, social and economic problems became more complex. In turn, rural America was portrayed as simpler and nobler than urban areas. Never mind that frontier life oftentimes was a desperate existence, or that many fledgling towns deserved their reputations for lawless depravity. In the popular, if not philosophical, national mind-set, rural America offered a wholesome alternative to the "tendency of city life to corrupt the very young." Settlers reinforced this view. As one woman explained it, her family had left the rapid urbanization of the East "because of the pitfalls there for our sons: temptation awaited them everywhere, and we dared not stay."[18]

People were propelled toward the Great Plains for a number of reasons. Explicitly stated or not, the message was oftentimes that the move was made to benefit the children. Parents saw themselves laying a foundation for a future in which children would be better off economically and socially. The American Dream was clearly acted out in the West when settlers expected self-improvement and achievement, if not for themselves, for the next generation.

Expectations and Realities

Youngsters approached their new homes with any number of expectations. Many were fueled by parental hopes. Joshua Wheatcroft clearly echoed his parents when he called western Kansas "the land of opportunity." Other expectations were based on what youngsters read or were told. One young girl, bound for Kansas at the time of the well-publicized grasshopper plagues, anticipated living on a diet of grasshopper soup. Many youngsters believed they would see buffalo and Indians. Harry Colwell, a thirteen-year-old orphan sent west by the New York Children's Aid Society, anticipated "cowboys and Indians, a chance to ride horses and to participate in all sorts of exciting adventures." By the time he arrived in 1898, however, Indians were on reservations and his adventures were restricted to a typical turn-of-the-century rural center. In fact, by the time most settlers and town builders arrived in the latter half of the 1800s, neither buffalo nor Indians were common sights.[19]

Location and time period determined both the context and response to Native Americans. Alma Carlson, who arrived in Nebraska in the 1880s, when tribal groups had been removed to reservations, thought it was the "Indians [who] needed protection from the whites"—not the other way around. Fannie Cole was ambivalent. She and her family, especially older members who were "fervent admirers of J. Fenimore Cooper's Indian stories," looked forward to seeing Delaware Indians on their Kansas reserve. Nothing, however, could live up to literary descriptions, and a disappointed Fannie dismissed the tribe as "homely." Youngsters such as Alma and Fannie were observers, unlike missionary children or those at military posts who either had daily contact with Native Americans or participated in routines that revolved around their presence. At Fort McPherson, Rachel Lobach and her sister believed that Native Americans watched them with "great curiosity." James

Walker, whose father was employed at the Fort Berthold Indian Agency, recalled that native men and women around the agency "were very fond of my baby brother. They constantly played and talked with him to such an extent that the first word my brother said was the Arikara word for no, 'Kokee.' "[20]

After the Civil War the federal government intensified its resolve to place Native Americans on reservations. Settlers, town builders, and railroad companies wanted the land, but the tribes of the plains did not simply acquiesce. In 1868 and 1869, for example, military campaigns in Kansas and Nebraska brought reprisals and a wave of fear among the white population. In 1868 a number of settlers in western Kansas were killed when Kiowas, Comanches, and Cheyennes attempted to stave off the railroads and settlement. "The women and children," wrote one man, "are in constant terror." Six years later, members of a survey party were killed; among the victims was fourteen-year-old Daniel Short, who was accompanying his father. Probably the most talked-about incidents, and those that increased Westerners' fears and demands for reprisals, were those that involved families. In 1854 news of an overland party of men, women, and children killed near Fort Boise (Idaho) spread eastward along the Oregon-California Trail and back to the new territories of Kansas and Nebraska. Twenty years later the ambush of a family on its way to Colorado reignited old fears. The parents and three of the children (two girls and one boy) were killed, but four girls, from seventeen to five years of age, were taken captive. After a military contingent gave pursuit, the two oldest girls were rescued, and four months later the younger girls were returned when a group of Cheyennes agreed to go to a reservation.[21]

Parents reassured children of protection while making little attempt to shield them from stories of attack and conflict. It was for their own safety, adults reasoned, that youngsters know the possible dangers. Adult fears that Indians wanted to steal white children were translated at military posts into rules that forbade youngsters from venturing beyond fort boundaries without an escort. Rachel Lobach and her sister were "practically . . . raised" on stories of Indian attacks and sternly warned to stay near the barracks for fear that "the Indians might carry us off." Although Rachel seemed to shake off such concerns, seven-year-old Minnie Severson in Nebraska was much more impressionable. Minnie was not a post resident. There was no safe garrison to protect her. After the military's massacre of Indian men, women, and children at Wounded Knee, rumors of reprisals terrified Minnie, and she spent sleepless nights imagining that Indians were coming for her. Mary Leefe was all too familiar with threats of attacks. She and other post children sometimes had their hair cropped "as close as billiard balls," presumably to make them less attractive targets for scalping. "I myself wore a boy's haircut up to my sixteenth birthday," she recalled. Reassured by her parents that the garrison offered protection, Mary did not dwell on what might happen. She could not, however, erase her first memory, as a six-year-old, of Fort Dodge (Kansas) and a blood-splattered blanket that marked the commander's death at the hands of Indians. Years later she wrote: "It has taken many years for those of us who were children of the old army to overcome the dread and hatred we had for the Indians of those days." It was nearly impossible to understand that injustices were perpetrated against Native Americans and that they feared for their own children at the hands of Euro-Americans.[22]

For both Mary Leefe, who saw a number of frontier posts, and James Walker at Fort Berthold, Indian-white relations were sometimes confusing and contradictory. While at Fort Garland (Colorado) in 1881, Mary and other children were allowed to visit encamped White River Utes. The prospect "sent galloping shivers down our spines. . . . Now we were to see these terrible foes at first hand!" Incompatible with these feelings was the visit itself, which turned into a politely orchestrated social occasion. Each youngster carried a cotton bag filled with marbles, beads, pencils, and bubble pipes made of clay as gifts for the children of the "terrible" enemy. Clearly separating friend from foe was not always easy, as James Walker well knew. He played with Indian boys his age and they taught him their language, but he avoided them if there were more than two or three. "They would become abusive and try to see how badly they could scare me." In the world of children, aggressive behavior is not unusual, and clearly the boys knew and played on Walker's fears. On one occasion when James and his friend George Alden, son of the Indian agent, were together, "We were ambushed in very real fashion by a dozen or more boys. . . . They beat us with sticks and shot arrows very close to us . . ."[23]

Most children only heard about Indians. Contact with people who were somehow "different" most often occurred within the disparate mix that made up Western society. Eleven-year-old Julia Cody, traveling from Iowa to Kansas, saw African Americans for the first time and was afraid of them. Her younger brother William (later famous as "Buffalo Bill") was less fearful and more curious, wondering "if they were Indians or were like the Indians we would see in Kansas Territory." Jennie Elizabeth Milton also recorded seeing the unusual—"Lots of Negros" and one "Chinaman." When new neighbors or fellow travelers differed in appearance, language, or behavior, they were met with caution. Among immigrant groups, the Germans from Russia came in for a large share of comment. Numerous newspaper correspondents took particular pains to explain that Germans from Russia represented two groups, the Mennonites and the Catholic Volga Germans. Stories varied in tone. More than one commented on homespun clothing worn by women and children and the "funny old handkerchiefs tied round their heads." There was open ridicule, but the overriding intent of newspaper stories was to introduce Germans from Russia as good citizens who arrived with ready cash and stern determination. One Nebraska newspaper informed readers that Mennonites were stoop-shouldered because they were so industrious.[24]

Perhaps bewildered by their new surroundings, recently arrived Russian immigrants stand for a photograph in Yankton, South Dakota. *(South Dakota State Historical Society)*

Characteristics attributed to any group surely influenced young people's behavior and attitudes. George MacGinitie never knew why Bohemians in his Nebraska neighborhood were considered inferior by non-Bohemians, but he understood the rules of us-versus-them. He and one particular Bohemian boy "got along wonderfully well," but "when some of the town boys were looking I, of course, had to pretend that I didn't like him." Charles Driscoll, himself a target for prejudice because he was Irish Catholic, easily adopted attitudes he heard voiced against "foreigners," which in this case meant Germans in general. "I understood . . . [the man] will spend all the money on implements to make work easier for him in the fields . . . leaving his poor wife and daughters to slave away in the house with an old-fashioned stove and no pump." Lettie Little described the "foreign ways" of Germans, although she had no firsthand contact. The immigrants made wine, ate large quantities of sauerkraut, and "their women even worked in the field. . . . It was said that even their babies came easier."[25]

Consciously or not, youngsters made comparisons between themselves and new neighbors. Ovella Dunn, reared in a fairly well-to-do household and accustomed to the social rituals demanded by polite society, discovered that young women in the new state capital of Topeka, Kansas, were not "punctual in calling on strangers." Ovella excused the breach in etiquette only because it was impossible to keep up with expected courtesy visits with "so many strangers coming in all the time." Customs and appearance both came in for their share of comment. Fourteen-year-old William Lewis, new to the Texas Panhandle in 1885, saw boys no older than himself wearing neckerchiefs and wide-brimmed hats. These were "cowboy" clothes worn by the real thing. His great excitement was considerably dampened, however, when he realized that when his peers looked at him, they saw a newly arrived Easterner laughably dressed in knickerbockers with long black stockings, a ruffled shirt, and a sailor hat with ribbon streamers. An embarrassed William was then completely humiliated when his mother put him in charge of carrying the birdcage.[26]

Perceptions

Youngsters arrived with a host of preconceived notions and expectations. These in turn influenced responses to the realities of the natural environment and the demanding process of settlement. Perceptions were also shaped by place of birth. Children who migrated to the plains from somewhere else never quite saw their new environment in the same way as those who were born in the West. Bob Kennon, the son of Texas pioneers, was born and reared in the state, and that was his point of reference. "We loved our home dearly," he wrote. "Texas was a land of vast expanses, free land, countless ways to make money in the livestock game." Transplanted children, on the other hand, quite naturally compared new surroundings to what they had known. Ovella Dunn considered Kansas and decided that she would not "exchange my situation here for the handsomest residence in Zanesville [Ohio] no not for the world." Fresh from New York State, Bertie Canfield described anything unusual on the Kansas prairies as "funnie": the post office in a dugout "was a funnie place," and the landscape without any fences looked "very funnie to us." New York and Kansas were different, but Bertie was enthusiastic and quite willing to adapt. "The longer we stay the better we like it."[27]

Of course, not everyone immediately took to new surroundings. The Dorsey family was more typical of newcomers that slowly acclimated. Until a claim was located, a lack of accommodations in Nebraska City forced the family to live in a dismal one-room structure. It was a poor start, and eight-year-old Will threw himself on the floor crying that he would never live in such a stable. Everyone's outlook improved, however, when the family moved into a cabin on a Nemaha River claim. "Soft zephyrs floated o'er us, bright flowers gave out their perfume, and all nature was glad," wrote daughter Mollie.[28]

George Thompson also needed a period of adjustment. He spent his "first few days" in Nebraska being scared. A number of prairie fires were "too close for comfort," and the "nerve racking howls of the coyotes" kept the boy awake for hours at night. Fifteen-year-old Carrie Schmoker was skeptical that southwestern Kansas would ever be to her liking. There was "not a single home, fence, field, or tree, nothing but the brown trail. . . . On the high flats we saw a few prairie dog towns." No "soft zephyrs" or wildflowers lured acceptance.[29]

Responses were individual and subjective. While some youngsters reacted with reserve or doubt, any number described their first sight of the plains with awe. Marian Sloan wrote about the play of sunlight on the prairie and "haunting, unearthly, and lovely" sunsets. Joshua Wheatcroft did not see the expected buffalo and Indians, but he was far from disappointed. "From the first day I first set eyes on western Kansas there was something about this new country that appealed to me."[30] George MacGinitie was unabashedly lyrical remembering his introduction to his Nebraska home.

> At one place our covered wagon moved slowly over the crest of a ridge and there before us as far as the eye could see stretched the width of the Niobrara River, shining like silver in the sun and disappearing in the distant blue haze. The sight thrilled me so deeply that, although I was only two years old at the time, I have never forgotten it.[31]

Towns received comment too. When William Lewis and his family detrained at Harrold, Texas, the town was "in its most primitive stage. . . . The only wooden structures were the hotel, the saloon, and the cattle pens." Residents and businesses made do with tents. Time and place decided what newcomers encountered at a prairie town. In its early days, for example, Kearney, Nebraska, was described as a rough place populated by the "worshippers of Bacchus and the Dealers of cards." By 1876, however, the town's raucous days were a memory, and a Swedish settler on his first visit to Kearney found that the "notoriously hard town" was an "enterprising" place with rail service, churches, stores, banks, and a school. Many of the buildings, noted the settler, were "of brick and quite pretentious."[32]

Children's perceptions and outlooks could not help but be colored by those of their parents. This seemed to be especially true of the mother's response. Some women celebrated the prairies and the possibilities for new opportunities. One Kansas woman wrote that hardships were offset by "the attraction of the prairie, which simply gets into your blood and makes you dissatisfied away from it." Others found adjustment more difficult. When Wilianna Hickman and her husband arrived at Nicodemus, a Kansas town established by former slaves, she saw the dugouts, the "uninviting" scenery, and "I began to cry." Agnes Krom was a young girl who saw western Kansas through her mother's eyes. It was a "great barren waste." Another girl concluded that her mother "never became quite satisfied with Kansas," though she made a brave attempt to "brighten up" and hide her feelings from the children. Still, many a child recognized homesickness and a reluctance to relocate. As the Siceloff family headed to Oklahoma's Cherokee Strip, "[mother] kept looking back, despair in every line of her face." Although the family's new home was only thirty-five miles from "settled" Kansas, she had crossed a psychological boundary between civilization and the unsettled West.[33]

What areas were settled and no longer a part of the American frontier was a point of debate in the late 1800s. Frontier conditions remained long past the time a place was "settled" and long after the 1890 U.S. Census indicated that there was no longer a "frontier line," meaning that no geographical marker such as a river or mountain range conclusively separated the settled from unsettled. By the late 1800s, children grew up in three general types of environments: frontier conditions that continued in sparsely populated areas and in those just opening to settlement; rural areas that were past the homesteader stage; and a new, emerging urban West of small towns and growing cities. By the end of the century, there were striking differences. While Nebraskan George MacGinitie and his peers watched a town's thrilling Fourth of July reenactments of Indian raids on mail stages and felt nostalgia for what they had missed by being born late in the century, fourteen-year-old Clara Ewell needed no choreographed demonstration of what the frontier might have been. Spending her first night on the family's Cherokee Strip claim, Clara sensed her participation in a historic moment.

"We built a campfire and ate our meager supper. At nightfall, we could see the other campfires and lights. The music of guitars and singing could be heard instead of the hooting owl and howling coyote. Thus civilization in a new country was started."[34]

CHAPTER TWO

Travel and Settlement

—————

✒ IRA THOMAS WAS TEN YEARS OLD when his family left Iowa for Sioux County, northwest Nebraska.

> We arrived on Thanksgiving Day in the year 1888. The trip was approximately 600 miles. We traveled in a covered wagon drawn by a team of mules and it took us 43 days to make the trip. Everything we owned was in the wagon and my parents had the total sum of $25.00. Our party included my mother, father, and five children—Theresa, Charlie, myself, Harry, and Sam.[1]

This description nicely fits the popular perception of a homesteading family setting off on its own to establish a home in the American West. In actuality, people arranged themselves in a number of ways for travel and settlement. In 1870 ten-year-old Percy Ebbutt left England with his father, a twelve-year-old brother, and three young men who were not related but interested in "the far west of America." Traveling by ship and then by train from New York to the "far west," which for them was north central Kansas, the four men and two boys "moved up on the prairie with our luggage, and boards to build our house" in February 1871. There was no single approach to reaching the plains. Some children arrived with only their immediate family while others made the trip in groups of varying sizes and makeup. The Ebbutt party was fairly typical of migrants who banded together for safety, mutual aid, and social contact.[2]

Some traveling partnerships were loosely arranged affairs, but thousands of homesteaders and town builders came to the plains in organized "colonies." Those originating within the United States usually sent a small party of men ahead to investigate prospective sites, choose a place for settlement, and make arrangements for the group's arrival. Meanwhile, those left behind pooled resources and occasionally solicited donations from friends or local organizations. Colonies were regionally, culturally, and racially diverse. The Johnson family was one of nine Swedish families that left Illinois for Nebraska, and the Gills were part of what became known as the Hodgeman County Colony, a group of former slaves that settled in southwestern Kansas. The Pearlette Colony, named for a young girl who died soon after the group's arrival in Kansas, consisted of sixteen Caucasian families from Ohio. Pearlette Colony members, much like other colonists, either combined a portion of their money or paid a fee to offset the expense of travel and shipment of goods. It was a cost-effective plan that allowed people to share resources rather than take on the burden of migration alone.[3]

A number of colonization plans were developed by for-profit land companies. Even before the Dakotas achieved territorial status, Minnesota and Iowa speculators organized land companies with designs on an area that would become part of South Dakota. The Kansas Land and Emigration Company, established in 1869, focused on bringing British families to a settlement called Wakefield, and in the Texas Panhandle, the family of William Lewis settled in Clarendon, a Methodist settlement established by a minister with British investors backing the town colony and surrounding ranch. Speculators understood that town and agricultural development were interdependent.

Promotional materials not only promised good farmland but highlighted the refinements of developing towns. Some towns were advertised through elaborately printed maps or lithographs illustrating businesses, churches, and schools—as yet to be built. Fannie Cole's extended family was drawn to a town in territorial Kansas that "had been laid out by some southern gentlemen, and on paper it was an imposing city." In reality it boasted one log residence and a single store. More than one townsite was proclaimed to be the new "Gateway to the West" or promised to be the future site of a county seat, college, or state capital. In the fierce competition to woo investors and residents, some towns never existed anywhere but on paper. "Land speculation," wrote a horrified Horace Greeley, "is about the only business in which a man can embark with no other capital than an easy conscience. . . . The speculators in broadcloth are not one whit more rapacious or pernicious than the speculators in rags, while the latter are forty times the more numerous."[4]

Before the Civil War, foreign-born migrants moved to the plains for a number of reasons, including the enticement of colonization schemes, but it was not until the 1870s and 1880s that immigrants arrived in large numbers. These fell into two broad categories: those who traveled from some other part of the United States, and those who came directly from England, Ireland, Wales, Scotland, the German states, or the Scandinavian countries. There were also Germans from Russia as well as people from France, the Netherlands, Belgium, Bohemia (Czechs), and Canada. By the late 1800s, populations from eastern and southern Europe and Mexico arrived. The latter, in particular, were encouraged to come to the Central Plains to work for railroad companies or in sugar beet production.

Migration out of Europe played a large role in peopling the plains, and place of origin is recalled today in the names given to towns and villages—Bavaria, Glasco, Denmark, Munich, Geneva, Scotland. Problems within home countries encouraged emigration, and American railroads exerted a strong external influence. Railroads had a vested interest in promoting settlement and, by extension, their own commerce. Immigrants were potential buyers of railroad lands, and when these were lined with farms and towns, rail companies anticipated additional income from goods shipped to market. After the American Civil War, strategies that had proved successful in promoting Western settlement within the United States were also used in Europe. Broadsides and booklets were printed in several languages and widely distributed. No matter the language, the promises were the same. The Great Plains had sufficient rainfall, mild winters, a healthy climate, and unbounded agricultural possibilities. Just as important, fears of being isolated by language were groundless. Said a German-language publication, "He [the immigrant] will find many neighborhoods just as German as the one he left in the old country." To further sell immigration, railroad companies hired agents to travel abroad, make personal contacts, and facilitate travel by ship and then by rail from ports of entry.[5]

Supporting these efforts were immigrants already in the West; foreign-language newspapers; ethnic-religious groups such as the Irish Catholic Colonization Society, the Swedish Agricultural Company, and the Hebrew Union Agricultural Society; and immigration bureaus established by territorial and state governments. South Dakota's territorial legislature named a commissioner of immigration who was responsible for nothing else than publicizing the Dakotas. By 1875 these efforts were superseded by a legislatively mandated bureau of immigration which published promotional material in several languages and sent representatives to meet immigrants at port cities. Potential settlers were faced with a barrage of booster rhetoric and personal appeals to come to the plains. Once travelers left their homelands and reached the United States, aid societies helped them along or, as in the case of Dakota representatives, steered them toward a particular area. Railroads completed the process by transporting the newcomers in "emigrant" cars at special fares; freight, including agricultural implements, was shipped at affordable rates. The "fruits of this foreign immigrant work," wrote the commissioner of emigration for the Atchison, Topeka & Santa Fe Railway, "[were] the prosperous German, Austrian, Swiss and Mennonite settlements [on the] Santa Fe system." Meanwhile the Northern Pacific Bureau of Immigration was credited for North Dakota's influx of Scandinavians, Russian Jews, and Germans from Russia.[6]

Most colonies from Europe were made up of people who had known each other before immigration. Extended families, friends and neighbors, and, sometimes, whole villages relocated together. Often they combined resources. Recalled a member of a Prussian colony: "When we decided to go to Texas, we put all our savings in a common treasury, part of which we invested in buying things we thought necessary to start a settlement. Our intention was to buy a tract of land to be held in common, and later to locate our individual claims." As might be expected, settlers usually discovered that promotional descriptions, as well as what they imagined the West to be, were off the mark. Before arriving in Texas, two brothers pictured "pioneer life as one of hunting and fishing, of freedom from the restraints of Prussian society." They never considered that it also meant "drudgery and toil." Christine Hinderlie, who had her tenth birthday while onboard the steamship transporting her from Norway to America, lived first in Minnesota. Then the family moved to "deathly scary" South Dakota. Would-be settlers were best advised, wrote a Norwegian immigrant in North Dakota, to "consider the matter twice before you leave the Fatherland and the place where your cradle stood. It is not a small matter."[7]

Group travel had its benefits, including access to lodging during that critical period when the destination was reached but claims had not yet been filed and homes built. In many instances, local communities or government agencies or railroads provided temporary housing. South Dakota's Bureau of Immigration saw that buildings were constructed at Yankton to house European arrivals while homestead claims were filed. Mennonites gathered at the fair-grounds in Lincoln, Nebraska, and the Santa Fe Railroad housed Mennonites in Topeka, Kansas. Topeka was also a gathering point during the mass migration of African Americans into the state in 1879 and 1880. Since these "exodusters" arrived with little or no money, they required both shelter and the aid provided by the Freedman's Relief Association organized by the state's governor. Willingness to assist with housing and aid underscores the competition that raged between sections of the plains for permanent residents who, in turn, would develop an area's agricultural, business, and cultural resources.[8]

Of course, most settlers did not receive aid or board at public or private expense. The Pearlette Colony planned fairly well, but when the sixteen families detrained at Dodge City, Kansas, they had not enough money for everyone to stay in a hotel while claims were located and filed. Improvising on the spot, the colonists bought enough lumber to construct a small haphazard structure that temporarily housed the settlers and their belongings. A teenage boy in the party recalled, "beds covered the whole of each side of the shanty—the goods piled in the center—each family in a group." Less fortunate was a group that arrived in the Solomon River Valley of Kansas just before a snowstorm hit. Without housing, the new arrivals lived in wagons with little to eat and only wagon canvas as protection against the elements. The "suffering among the women and children, particularly, is very severe," a local newspaper editor wrote, reporting the settlers' plight with a shake of the head. "It is a mystery why people will push out to the frontier, at the commencement of winter. We admire their pluck, but can hardly commend their discretion." Still, homesteaders often arrived during inclement weather. Joshua Wheatcroft was twelve years old when he and his family arrived in western Kansas with three wagons that carried them and all their worldly goods. "But it was winter and we were out on the open prairies, without a house, barn, or well." Until sod could be broken and a house built, the wagons afforded the only shelter. Catherine Wiggins and her brother Sam would have almost preferred winter cold to the heat they endured before a home was constructed. Wrote Catherine: "The sun shone as only a Kansas sun can shine. There was no shade save that of the tent and the tent grew unbearably hot . . . and I, although a big girl, eleven years old, proved myself a poor sport, crying because I was thirsty."[9]

Rail travel from port cities was common for European arrivals, but no single mode of transportation represented the experience of migrants moving out of Eastern and Southeastern states. Some traveled exclusively by wagon, perhaps using rail service only to ship agricultural equipment and household goods to a depot closest to the final destination. Other would-be Westerners used more than one type of transportation. It took the Dorsey family two weeks to travel by train, ferry, and riverboat from Indiana to Nebraska Territory. The boat trip up the Missouri River was an especially pleasant experience for everyone. "I never had a better time," wrote Molly. Bertie Canfield, headed for Kansas, and William Lewis, destined for the Texas Panhandle, began their journeys by rail. So did eleven-year-old Mary Leefe, who was on her way to Fort Ringgold (Texas). Trains could take them only so far, however. The final leg of Bertie's trip was made by wagon; William's was by stage; Mary and her family covered the last ninety miles "in an army ambulance and escort wagon across a vast expanse of sand, cactus, scrub oak, and mesquite."[10]

From accounts left by those who made the journey west, it is clear that families did not always travel together. Army dependents usually followed, rather than accompanied, officers and troops, and many homesteading families went through periods of separation. In the spring of 1879 Jessie Shepard and her two sisters stayed behind in New York State while their parents went ahead to Kansas; by the time the girls followed in the fall of that year, a sod house was waiting to welcome them. Other youngsters reported fathers who went ahead to stake a claim. "My mother, with her four small children, came to Laramie County, Wyoming Territory, in July, 1884, . . . my father having come in the spring and found a location southwest of Lusk," recalled Maggie Pfister, who was four years old at the time of the move. Many homeseekers were steered toward a particular place by acquaintances already there; Maggie's uncle, for example, was at least partially responsible for the family choosing Wyoming. Colonization companies or land promoters influenced other settlers. One boy recalled that his father was advised by a promoter to head for southwestern Kansas: "This part of the country was beginning to outgrow its wildness, and buffalo had about disappeared, the Indians were reasonably quiet, and the soldiers at Fort Dodge, being so near, promised protection from any further raids." Another youngster was sure that her father and two male relatives were tricked by "unscrupulous land agents" who directed them to a place with "natural springs" that, it turned out, were only temporarily filled buffalo wallows.[11]

As single families and colonies selected locations for settlement, they created a checkerboard across the Great Plains that reflected racial, religious, and national diversity. The West was filled with a multiplicity of cultures. By 1890 most youngsters in North Dakota were the children of immigrants, and the population in southeastern South Dakota was predominantly immigrant—Norwegian, Swedish, Danish, Bohemian, and Germans from Russia. Mennonites were the majority in some central Kansas counties while Volga Germans constituted the largest population in a few of the state's western counties. When racism was encountered, some African Americans, including those in what became South Dakota's Sully County Colored Colony, responded by selecting places where there were few whites. In other areas, groups of specific ethnic or racial backgrounds settled together in small clusters. Most homesteaders in Sheridan County, Kansas, for example, were American-born

Caucasians, but there was one pocket of settlers from the Nether-lands and another from Ireland.[12]

The westering experience of immigrant children and, to a lesser degree of African Americans, was shaded by the homogenous environment of transplanted communities. African-American families passionately intended to break free of a slave past by establishing and maintaining social, religious, and familial structures. For their part, immigrant groups retained cultural frameworks that, at least for the first generation, went unchallenged. Children defined themselves and events in their lives in terms of those around them. They sang the old songs, celebrated special days in traditional ways, and spoke the language of their parents. Immigrants replicated the social and educational institutions they had left behind, and it was possible to keep abreast of events, as well as people "back home," through native-language newspapers. There was little reason to quickly assimilate into a larger society when everyone in the immediate vicinity shared the same language and cultural touchstones. Indeed, it is one of America's myths that immigrants rushed to join the dominant culture. In both towns and rural settings, traditional life was maintained, and children developed ethnic, racial, and religious identities that bound them to a common past and a cohesive present.

Settling In

Reaching their final destinations, homesteaders faced a multitude of tasks. Breaking the prairie for crops and gardens (an acre of sod a day was typical), caring for livestock, filling larders with game, wild greens, and fruit, and building shelter for both humans and live-stock demanded immediate attention. Among the most critical problems was finding water. Very few settlers or town residents immediately dug wells. Hand digging was potentially dangerous, and in many areas the cost was prohibitive if it meant drilling down hundreds of feet. Typically, water was hauled from the closest source. "A well in those days had to be dug by hand and to go down 150 feet or better in this fashion was no easy matter," recalled a Kansan who as a boy of seven, with a twelve-year-old brother, hauled barrels of water from a creek five miles away. Over time, however, plains residents dug wells, built windmills to draw water, and added water-catching gutters (leading to a rainwater barrel). The Singley family hauled water for seven years before digging a well. "It was a big job," wrote daughter Rosetta, remembering the depth, 150 feet, and the dangers of cave-ins.[13]

Housing construction was sometimes delayed until crops and gardens were in the ground. When building began, style was greatly influenced by finances, available building materials, and the landscape. "In the matter of buildings they have been guided more by necessity," wrote a Danish pioneer in North Dakota. Both immigrants and American-born homesteaders found it difficult, if not impossible, to immediately replicate familiar building methods and architecture. Where there was an abundance of lumber, settlers built the typical frontier log cabin or shanty. Percy Ebbutt's shanty home "was certainly none too large, though, for six of us, . . . and it was so low that no one could stand upright in it at the highest part."[14] The log cabin occupied by Nebraskan Will Cox during the early 1860s was built in starts and stops as the family concentrated on breaking ground and planting crops and garden.

> Sometime in August we occupied our new 'residence.' . . . Of course our house was incomplete: bed sheets hung over the openings instead of glass windows, cracks between the logs were chinked but not plastered but it was surely home sweet home compared with living outdoors for nearly five months.[15]

Where timber was scarce and lumber shipment costly, building materials were adapted from the natural environment. Houses and outbuildings were constructed of adobe or native limestone, and in some places the A-frame "hay house" (horizontal ribbing covered with prairie grass) served as the first home. The sod house, however, came to symbolize adaptive use of what was available. Constructed of sod cut from the prairie with a "breaking plow," the sod house or soddie was formed by blocks or "bricks" of sod placed in staggered layers (grass side down). Openings were left for doors and windows, and the roof was supported by a ridge pole that rested on forked posts placed at either end of the house. Some roofs were finished with shingles or boards, but this was more expensive than a natural sod covering that sprouted native grasses and wildflowers during spring and summer. Inside these homes, walls were sometimes left in a natural state, but it was more common to plaster or cover with paper. One Norwegian boy recalled that his family's Dakota soddie was decorated with the pages of the *Decorah-Posten* and *Skandinaven* newspapers.[16]

Less time was needed to construct a dugout, which was just what the name suggested. On the open prairie, a dugout was simply a hole dug about six feet deep with sod walls constructed about three feet above ground. Where there was a hillside or outcropping, the dugout was cut out, with the exposed side covered with sod, brush, or other available material. Clara Ewell's first home on a Cherokee Strip claim "was dug into a bank. Part of the walls and the floor were dirt, but the A-roof was made with shingles." The story was the same elsewhere. Norwegian settlers at Lake Hendricks, South Dakota, in 1873 lived in wagons while they dug homes out of a hillside. In Kansas, the first African Americans to arrive at the townsite of Nicodemus "quickly learned to build dugouts," though some newcomers tried lean-tos before experience taught them that structures of sapling and canvas could not withstand strong prairie winds. Most African Americans in another Kansas colony, Hodgeman, built sod houses, with the exception of the Gill family whose house came in for special comment. "It was a curiosity," recalled a woman more than fifty years later. "[It was] part dug-out part sod, with a roof of tin, made of tomato cans with the ends melted off."[17]

Newcomer reactions to individual house forms varied from disbelief to amusement. Rachel Calof, a Jewish emigré from Russia, was appalled by the lack of privacy in the small North Dakota structure that was to be her home, and a sixteen-year-old watched his mother's horror fade to acceptance when she first saw the family's Kansas dugout. The only thing separating the inside from the great outdoors was a canvas sheet. George C. Anderson, scouting prospective settlement sites for the Ohio Soldiers Colony, was struck by the variety of possibilities when he visited Kansas, Colorado, Wyoming, and Indian Territory. In one place he visited a family in "a very comfortable" two-story stone dwelling; in another he happened upon a homestead colony from Wisconsin "living in holes dug in the ground, which were covered with sheets and blankets." In a third place, he recorded a home "dug in the side of a hill, with trenches around the top to keep the water from running into it. . . . The front of this palatial residence, was composed of a cotton sheet, for the purpose of keeping out the sun, rain, wind and burglars." A number of houses were more than private dwellings. One of the first homes in Bottineau, North Dakota, was described as "a fairly good sized tar-papered house which had a triple use—a postoffice, a little store and . . . home with a bed or two for travelers."[18]

Shelter was essential, but a structure was also necessary for meeting the homestead law's requirement for making "improvements" and living on the claim. Occasionally interpretation of the law was pushed to the limit. Usher Burdick's family lived in town during the first year in North Dakota, but about twice a week they walked to the homestead and stayed all night in their improvement of a tar-paper shanty. In Nebraska's Sandhills, Mary O'Kieffe and her oldest son took adjoining homesteads and built half of a soddie on his claim and half on hers. In western Kansas, four men put up a tar-paper shack at the point where their quarter sections met. During the winter of 1878 the shack, measuring sixteen by thirty-two feet, housed three families. Bunk beds were arranged along one wall, with curtains between for family privacy. The shack had no interior insulation such as lath or plaster, and one stove provided the only heat. Despite the crowded conditions and the miserable cold, each family technically met the obligation of improving and living upon its individual claims.[19]

Many homesteaders lived in sod houses for years or made a variety of additions to the structure. Dugouts, on the other hand, were often abandoned after the initial settlement phase. Adelia Clifton's family found dugout living almost unbearable during the summer. "We made brush arbors and dragged our beds outside . . . to sleep in the open at night." Limited living space was another practical consideration. In South Dakota a Norwegian family with twelve children turned the dugout into a cellar by building a frame house over it, and the Mayer family, consisting of seven children ranging in age from two to twenty years old, lived in a dugout only as long as it took to build a home made of adobe. It was typical of those built by many immigrants—one structure that contained living space for the family and attached barn for livestock. At about the same time the Mayer family was at work, a group at Nicodemus constructed one sod house so that an expectant mother would have a proper place in which to give birth. A dugout did not suit the occasion.[20]

Children's lives revolved around their homes, resulting in a wealth of descriptions and personal memories. Floors might be dirt, swept and brushed to hardness, or wood flooring covered with rugs or pieces of carpet. Fabric partitions sometimes separated sleeping and living areas. Canvas sheets were tacked to soddie and dugout ceilings, catching dirt and insects that fell from above, and when it rained outside it was likely to rain inside. Families might have to haul water and periodically face droughts, but when it rained, dugouts flooded and water worked its way through the natural roofs of soddies. Driven out of their home by rain streaming inside, a Kansas woman and her children fled to a neighbor's dugout. "But before morning there was six inches of water in it, so we had to make another move." This time the shelter was a sheet of boards set against a stone wall.[21] Rosetta Singley's reminiscence of western Kansas was peppered with rain stories:

> [The dugout was] plastered with a mixture of light colored gypsum, which dried smooth and hard. The floor was plain mother earth, which mother found wasn't ideal, when her son Carl began to crawl, for often he was caked with mud. . . . It was during the first storm, that mother was sitting at the table writing a letter home and was not aware of the approaching storm, until water began coming through the roof of the dug out, which was dried out by the summer heat. She tried to catch the drip but soon it was coming through in streams, all over the roof. Soon water was standing all over the floor filling the holes that had been swept out since March. Practically everything was wet. . . .[22]

Other childhood memories revolved around "snakes, centipedes, spiders and other denizens of the Plains." Living in an Oklahoma dugout, Adelia Clifton wrote, "One day John Chitwood pointed to the roof above, and said, in a very calm tone, 'Miss Sara, there's a snake over your head!' And, sure enough, there was a little snake wiggling around in the brush." Hardly any family was without a snake-related story. Near the Kansas-Colorado line, the Germann children were "playing hide and seek with the baby, whom they hid behind a curtain in a corner cupboard." It was a game played many times, but on this occasion, "Mother heard the rattle of a snake, and sure enough, there it was right beside the baby." A thorough search discovered another snake "curled around the bed post." Many stories involving "denizens of the Plains" were told with humor, but there were frightening and repellent incidents.

Moving into an abandoned ranch house near Fort Davis (Texas), the Reynolds family discovered that some animal had been inside gnawing at the woodwork. "The sight of those glaring tooth marks" gave young Sally an "eerie feeling" that led her to imagine "many and all kinds of wild animals visiting us at nighttime." And Anne Ellis was reduced to tears "just at the sordidness of it all" when her mother stabbed a rat through the ceiling canvas and "blood dripped through." A frontier doctor left another account, referring to small creatures that plagued prairie homes: "It was mid-summer. Doors and windows were open. Insects were flying around the one kerosene lamp . . . so I did not realize why my delirious patient kept muttering, 'Take 'em away, paw, take 'em away.' Later I realized that bedbugs were feasting on his already depleted blood supply."[23]

The physical environment of Western homes provided challenges in sanitation, ventilation, and adequate living space. Material comforts varied from bare necessities to an abundance of goods. Youngsters' diaries and reminiscences suggest what families did and did not own, and a wealth of nineteenth-century photographs and drawings chronicle homes on the open plains and in developing towns. Posed for photographers, families surrounded themselves with the things that were important to them. Organs or pianos were moved outdoors for photo sessions. Animals, buggies, and farm equipment were brought into the frame. Interior images displayed the best room in the house and its material wealth. Photographs of recently built residences, especially those of Victorian style, often concentrated on the building rather than people. As documentary evidence, photographs offer a historical record of the material culture that varied substantially in quality and quantity among Westerners.

Some families began with very little, converting whatever they could find into utilitarian household items. Wooden boxes and pieces of lumber became cupboards and tables and chairs. Charley O'Kieffe in western Nebraska recalled crude furnishings in most

The photographer of this Nebraska image noted that "the young lady and mother wanted to prove they owned an organ" but did not "want to show the old sod house to friends back east." *(Solomon D. Butcher Collection, Nebraska State Historical Society)*

homes: "Nearly every item in the house, with the possible exception of a favorite rocking chair or bureau brought along on the trip west, was homemade out of native lumber with the accent on utility rather than beauty or grace." Other migrants brought substantial amounts of furnishings with them, and others came with little but were able to amass possessions over a period of time. The Pratt family, for example, were English immigrants who began with a small, two-room limestone house in western Kansas. As the family's sheep ranch prospered, money was spent to enlarge the house and purchase furnishings and decorations that could have been found in any comfortable urban home of the late Victorian era—stained-glass windows, mahogany furniture shipped from England, and a piano. It was the type of home environment that army dependents such as Mary Leefe would have easily recognized. Military families

The little girl in this southwest Kansas home shows off a doll and dollbed amidst the family's other possessions. *(Kansas State Historical Society)*

moved their possessions from place to place, and some Western posts offered fairly comfortable housing along officers' row. At Fort Dodge in the 1870s, the Leefes' parlor boasted lace curtains, wine-colored velvet drapes, a matching rug, a piano, and decorative vases on the mantle. At the other end of the spectrum, of course, were more primitive officers' housing at many frontier outposts and sub-standard quarters provided for married troopers and army laun-dresses (who were often married to enlisted men). At Fort Robinson (Nebraska), Caucasian and African-American families lived in twelve-by-thirty-five-foot quarters on "laundresses row," and at Fort Sill (Oklahoma), "company laundresses, together with troops of shock-headed children" inhabited "a [squalid] collection of huts, old tents, picket houses and dugouts."[24]

Urban Landscapes

The built environment created by town promoters and residents was part of the urban settlement movement of the Great Plains. Colony planners and town organizers designed settlements to reflect specific ideas of what a town should be and to attract residents who shared that vision. Immigrant groups laid out villages that both physically and culturally resembled those left behind, and Euro-American town builders intentionally tried to replicate familiar core businesses and desirable civil and social institutions. On the High Plains of Kansas, as one illustration, the town of Atwood was little more than an idea in 1879. Still, promoters and planners intended it to reflect respectable enterprise and moral values. It was advertised as a temperance town; "traffic in alcoholic liquors" would not be allowed. A schoolhouse was in the making, a "Presbyterian minister is already on the ground," and a Methodist circuit rider was on the way. Religion, temperance, and common school education signaled a place that welcomed solid businessmen and hardworking, churchgoing families. Saloonkeepers, prostitutes, and con men should look elsewhere.[25]

Some town builders saw the plains as a blank page that offered the unique opportunity of creating a "finished community" with tradesmen, specific industries such as milling, and a variety of social, educational, and religious institutions. Railroad companies laid out towns, fostering rapid urbanization in some places, but just as many towns were the result of private development. Individuals and private consortiums put up a hotel or general store in the hopes that a town would develop around them and attract rail lines. When rail routes went elsewhere, any number of villages failed or remained small, "inland" (away from the railroad) rural centers. Others refused to face defeat. Residents of Swan City, Nebraska, as one example, saw their town lose its status as a county seat and then fail to attract a railroad. The solution was to move "building, bed and baggage to the new town of DeWitt [on the rail line]." It was rather a shame, recalled Will Cox, who knew Swan City as a boy: "In its day [it] was considered a pretty decent burg. Never had a killin,' nor a jail."[26]

Of course, some towns and villages were not planned. They simply grew up around railroad construction, mining, military posts, or the cattle trade. "End-of-track" towns moved with rail construction; mining camps were easily abandoned; and the closing of a military post might mean the demise of a fledgling town. Some denizens of hastily created towns might imagine a permanent townsite in the future, but it was just as likely that most failed to see themselves as town builders. These towns were generally rough in appearance and character. Many had well-deserved reputations for rowdiness, lawlessness, and shady characters. Posted outside the cowtown of Wichita, Kansas, was a sign that read: "Everything goes in Wichita. Leave your revolvers at police headquarters." Wichita was not alone. Hays City, Kansas, attributed its existence to three primary entities—an army post, a railroad, and a railhead for cattle shipment. "There is a row of saloons on the Kansas Pacific railway called Hays City," wrote a journalist who visited the "fortress of sin" on July 4, 1871. "We should call it the Sodom of the plains."[27]

Less than fifteen years later a Fourth of July report from Hays City demonstrated just how much the town had changed from the days when there were "drunken fights in the street" and "[prostitutes] gave the scenes of violence rather a thrilling and terrible cast." On July 4, 1885, the big news was a new "skating hall" where "everyone took in the frolic and fun of the skating floor, as well as all the ice-cream and homemade they could conveniently hold. . . . [There was] not a jar or discord of any character to disturb the pleasure of the vast crowd."[28] The town was growing up. Countless other cow, military, and railroad towns did the same. The lawless image was suppressed to appeal to a broader, more sedate segment of the population.

Small towns and rural centers provided essential services while mirroring the surrounding agricultural community. Town residents usually had gardens, often raised chickens, kept horses, and had one or two cows. Businesses and professions were tied to the local economy, but by the latter half of the 1800s communities with only a few hundred residents looked to urban centers for inspiration and built public spaces such as parks and opera houses. Towns with substantial populations became centers for commerce, education, and government. This, in turn, meant paved streets (at least along main thoroughfares) and streetlights, landscaped parks, and theaters. Towns on the open plains initiated beautification projects, encouraging (and sometimes mandating) tree planting. Some places, bent on "progress," tried to emulate well-known metropolitan cities. Kearney, Nebraska, wanted to be "a new Chicago," and to prove the point boasted that its opera house was the largest between the Missouri River and Denver. At the close of the century, some municipalities had telephone service, water and sewage systems, and mechanized trolleys. Towns, both large and small, made a conscious transition from frontier to "civilized."[29]

The end of the century represented a golden age in small-town development and city refinements, but the plains did not shed its agricultural character. Most of residents still lived on farms in 1890, as did 65 percent of all American families. But the pattern was changing. During the 1880s and 1890s an emerging urban environment attracted farmers and ranchers away from the land. For the Beal family, the move from homestead to town in 1896 was a matter of the father going into business, but for the family it meant an end to isolation. "While living on the farm," wrote daughter Blanche, "Mama had been on the fringe of things. In Wichita [Kansas], she was in the middle of things. . . . [T]he whole family . . . was part of a real church with a regular preacher, a good graded Sunday school,

By the late 1800s, an increasing number of children were more familiar with town living than with rural life. *(Kansas State Historical Society)*

young people's groups, and women's societies." Other farm-to-town families moved to provide educational opportunities for their children, find more comfortable living conditions and social outlets, or earn better wages than provided by agriculture's boom-bust market economy. A small but persistent rural-to-urban migration began to redistribute the population, but a national decline in family farms and rural populations would not be noticeable for almost another twenty years when the U.S. Census of 1920 revealed that for the first time in the nation's history, the urban population outnumbered the rural.[30]

The emergence of small towns and growing cities separated childhood experiences into two broad categories: town kids and farm kids. They knew less and less about each other, and examined each other's worlds with a growing sense of distance. In the 1890s George MacGinitie saw his first electric lights and flush toilet when he visited the son of a prosperous merchant in Niobrara, Nebraska, and another boy's infrequent trips to Kimball, Nebraska, and Cheyenne, Wyoming, revealed such marvelous and unimagined things as "black 'rocks' which they used for fuel and called coal."

Towns exposed rural youngsters to all sorts of surprising things. The experiences, however, were events rather than part of everyday life.[31]

As a result, rural youngsters of the late 1800s made distinctions between themselves and the "citified." Lettie Little, for example, recalled a woman with "city ways" who moved into a farm community and gave a party—specifying that it was to last from three to five in the afternoon. "Setting the time to come was bad enough, but how could she have the nerve to tell them when to go home! Outlandish! Newfangled! Highbrow!" Comparisons were made and youngsters sometimes laughed at town folks, and conversely townspeople joked about country hicks. Watching "hay seeds mingle" was the way a town girl described an "old settlers" picnic in the early 1890s. Sniping aside, rural residents made a conscious effort to imitate some aspects of town life. By extension they were emulating American culture and social behavior. When Anne Ellis wanted a bustle, she improvised with an empty tomato can tied under her skirts, but the visual effect of "a lovely bustle" pleased the teenager's attempt at fashion in a Colorado mining camp. When the Driscoll children in Kansas decided to host a party, they turned to the columns of a national periodical for advice and sent formal invitations copied after a sample: "Yourself and Company are Cordially Invited." Part of the effort to learn and then act out social niceties was a desire to keep up, as best as possible, with the latest fashions and trends, but much of it stemmed from a desire to demonstrate cultural literacy and social aptitude.[32]

Rural youngsters had glimpses into town life and shared some of the same experiences in terms of education and social activities. They were less likely, however, to realize that town children faced social and cultural divisions. In developing cities, working-class families lived in different neighborhoods from the better off, and youngsters were quick to understand a pecking order determined by address. People of color were either segregated in public places or barred altogether. Both they and immigrant groups clustered in

Town residents, like these children clowning for the camera in whimsical hats, had numerous opportunities for social interaction and play activities. *(Kansas State Historical Society)*

specific neighborhoods, either because of restrictions imposed by outside forces or because of self-segregation. The larger the town, the more likely it was for children to realize that social stratums, prejudice, and economic barriers existed. There were, of course, exceptions, as Kate Chapman, an African-American teenager, illustrated in describing Yankton, South Dakota. In Yankton, she wrote, there was equality that in turn allowed the black community, with its own middle class of professionals, to prosper.[33] There was, in fact, an urbanized black population on the plains. Although the homesteading experience was still a strong presence in the lives of African Americans, immigrants, and American-born Caucasians, it shared a place with a growing urban environment that left its own lasting impressions on youngsters.

Town building and urbanization presented a paradox. American society idealized agrarian life and routinely warned against the dark side of urban living. On the other hand, towns, especially the small town, were increasingly touted as positive places for children. They provided educational and social opportunities that segregated children into groups by age. Social reformers and child-care experts of the late 1800s believed this beneficial. Although rural children had contact with their peers, youngsters in towns had more opportunities. This was, said fourteen-year-old Catherine Wiggins, the "bright spot" of moving from a claim to a small town. "I did get to meet and associate with people of my own age." In the ideal childhood of the late nineteenth century, children spent more time with peers than with adults. Town life made this possible by congregating children in a variety of activities that ranged from play visits to organized clubs. Rural children, on the other hand, lived in "a close association with parents, to the exclusion of outside interests." To some experts, this was a disadvantage: "The relationship may be very intense and personal, the parent's praise or blame becoming too highly significant to the child." American society began to reconsider its idealization of rural life and the family dynamics involved. These were small pinpricks, suggestive of subtle changes. Agrarian traditions remained strong, and the frontier spirit was considered an American characteristic, but an increasingly urban society began to tout the advantages of small-town living.[34]

CHAPTER THREE

Family and Community

―――――――――――

✟ MARY LEEFE spent much of her growing-up years on Western military posts. Her immediate family consisted of parents, a sister, two brothers, and maternal grandmother, but she considered herself to be a member of a larger group—the military family. There was a feeling, wrote Mary, "of being one family in the life of the post." The post family was made up of women and children, officers, enlisted men, servants, cooks, and tutors. It was not unusual for dependents, particularly officers' children, to describe themselves as part of this large military family. The idea was instilled by parents and reinforced by the circumstances of living, from post to post, in a self-contained, interdependent world that was a microcosm of social distinctions and rank.[1]

Military children were not alone in their sense of extended family and community. Nineteenth-century ideas about what made a family were elastic. Most American families were nuclear in structure but also inclusive. Family members and relatives, as well as servants, apprentices, intermittent hired workers, nursemaids, and tutors, could be counted among those making up a household and interacting with children on some level. This remained a family model during the 1800s, but as the century came to a close, Victorian standards and institutions enforced a social model that shifted to emphasize exclusivity. Fewer apprentices lived in the homes of instructors or employers; children were educated away from home rather than taught by tutors; and the gap widened between household employee and employer. As the white middle class of urban America increasingly shaped the standards of mainstream society, privacy of home and its interior life received new emphasis. The nuclear family shrank away from the outside world of urban growth, industrialization, and social ills.[2]

On the Western plains, family structure conformed to society's expectations, but it was less influenced by urbanization and more affected by the very act of settlement. When a nuclear family decided to head west, bonds with an extended family were broken. The same could be said for those traveling in colonies. Despite the probability that colonies comprised a network of kin, loved ones stayed behind. Some immigrant families came to the United States piecemeal, unable to afford passage for all at the same time. Migration and the plains experience itself altered relationships through mobility, multiple relocations, separation from "home," distances between Western homesteads, and the mix of humanity that gathered in new towns.

It was little wonder that the word "family" was applied to both the nuclear family and a community of neighbors and nonrelatives who seemed like "family." Youngsters understood their relationship to a nuclear family of kin, but they also spoke of military, community, or church families to which they belonged. "You see," wrote Lettie Little, "our religious activities were combined with our social life, and it was hard to tell where one left off and the other began." William Allen White agreed. For him, Sunday school was a social event that allowed time to be with others his own age and to enjoy the fun of trading good attendance cards for "marbles, chalk, and walnuts." Church, a place for spiritual uplift, brought neighbors and playmates together in the "family" activities of Christmas parties, ice cream socials, picnics, and church suppers. Members of a

Church gatherings, like this one in Nebraska in 1886, brought young and old together as an extended family. *(Solomon D. Butcher Collection, Nebraska State Historical Society)*

congregation sometimes referred to one another as "brother" and "sister," and ministers or priests acted as patriarchal head of family.[3]

For immigrants, the church maintained connections with a cultural past and served as a community center. In a few areas, only one religious group was present, but more commonly several were represented. Kingman County, Kansas, as illustration, had no "church edifices" in 1880, but the county's population of just over 3,700 represented six denominations—Baptist, Congregational, Episcopal, Methodist Episcopal, Presbyterian, and Roman Catholic. Some areas held community services as a "church family" until congregations constructed their own buildings, and in places such as Kingman County, denominations met in whatever was available—private homes, tents, saloons, schoolhouses, and shaded groves or brush arbors. "We met on the river and preaching was held under a brush arbor," recalled an Oklahoma resident. The place for observing the Sabbath was of less importance than its continued presence in the lives of settlers. "Our Sunday School was organized today," wrote a Kansas woman whose sod house was to be the meeting place. Church organization followed the same pattern in new towns. Services were held whenever and wherever possible until groups separated into discernible congregations, often with the help of missionaries such as the father of nine-year-old Frank Dean, who moved his wife and eight children to Steele City, Nebraska, where he established a church and farmed 80 acres. Mission work continued among Native Americans, but frontier communities presented a new challenge.[4]

Church and nuclear families blended together in a complex relationship of shared activities and religious beliefs. Daily prayers at home, Bible readings, and parental instruction reinforced church teachings. It seems that home activities reassured youngsters and drew the family together, but while children enjoyed the social aspects of church, sermons heard there were apt to bewilder and upset. Traveling preachers' literal interpretations of the Bible cast a pall over George MacGinitie's otherwise cheerful outlook. "I think I would have been much better off as a boy," he wrote, "without so much 'religion.' . . . I could not muster up the faith that I was supposed to have and without it I was sure I was lost." Charles Driscoll expressed much the same view when reflecting on his own shortcomings. "In a long and complicated series of computations, based upon the number and grievousness of my sins, I figured out my life span. I was going to drop dead while hoeing watermelons, at the age of 24." Confusion and fear were confronted in several ways. Older youngsters ridiculed preachers who exhibited more enthusiasm than religious training, and they winked at the emotional frenzy of religious camp meetings. Della Knowles used the meetings as pretext for having "quite a bit of fun" with her friends, and Percy Ebbutt described "the whole thing" as a weeklong picnic with "plenty to eat and drink and considerable amusement." Generally youngsters sorted out religion to their own satisfaction. Lettie Little thought it quite basic. Once you were baptized, there was a place in heaven. The only problem, she explained, was her mother, who "seemed to think that now we were Christian, [sister] Nellie and I ought not quarrel or fight. I couldn't see just why being right with God and Jesus should make me feel I should be nice to people."[5]

Church and the congregational family were strong and consistent influences, but it was only one type of family identified by children. Immigrant and African-American colonists considered themselves part of a community family, rather than families that inadvertently made up a community. Biological kinships and broadly constructed relationships tended to blur, leading children to accept nonrelations as an influential presence in their lives. A black resident in a Kansas town recalled: "Everybody looked after everybody's children. You didn't do anything that you got away with. Somebody told your parents." In countless places a neighbor woman was called "auntie" or "grandma" because she was the source of advice or help. Bachelor homesteaders, cowboys, hired hands, and enlisted soldiers filled roles that, in another place, would have been assumed by uncles, cousins, or even fathers. Marian Sloan and her brother Will thought that anything Santa Fe trader Francis Aubry did was "magical . . . [he] taught us many things on our long voyage across the Plains." On military posts, Mary Leefe and other children were "treated as pets [by] . . . grand old rugged veterans." In the Leefe household at Fort Dodge there was Johnson, an African-American cook adored by the children. "[We] were never so happy as when allowed to visit his quarters." Young people also found ways to establish long-distance relationships. When a Kansas woman proposed that women in her county "meet" once a week through a newspaper column because isolation kept them from regular socializing at church or school functions, a twelve-year-old, identifying herself as "Gazell," asked to be included. She was welcomed and invited to come "sit" in the "Home Corner" with women who were ready to offer advice and support. Thus, from an early age, children regarded themselves as members of a family group related by blood and as part of "families" bound together by religion, location, and shared experiences.[6]

Nuclear and extended families, and a strong sense of community, gave children a feeling of love, protection, and support. But these "families" never completely shielded youngsters from the seamier side of life. In the worst scenarios there were stories of abduction for prostitution or forced labor. In one of the former instances, a twelve-year-old Texas girl was kidnapped but rescued before being forced into prostitution. In a latter incident, a cowboy outfit lured a thirteen-year-old African-American boy to join them and then abandoned him in the Texas Panhandle. These were extreme examples of intentional threats to child safety and innocence. It was much more likely that adult behavior inadvertently influenced youngsters. By the age of fourteen, John Norton had seen his share of inebriated men at Fort Larned, and William Lewis in the Texas Panhandle was extremely curious about gaming tables in the local saloon, though he was not a frequent visitor. Guy V. Henry, Jr., and his sister preferred to imitate "Corporal Daugherty and Private McShane . . . [the] two worst men in the troops" when playing "soldier games," and Anne Ellis came face-to-face with less than respectable elements of society when she delivered laundry to a "fasthouse." Although warned by her mother never to go inside, she did. There was "a strong smell [of perfume] . . . [and] several pretty girls with lots of lace on their clothes, which were pretty loose affairs." The "fancy" women gave the girl candy, and she had "a very pleasant time."[7]

Intentionally or not, adults influenced and expanded the worldly education of young people. Even the most vigilant parents could not isolate youngsters from inviting temptations or adults who allowed youngsters to explore vices they considered harmless. John Ise told of older boys spending spare time at the home of an old bachelor where they learned to smoke, chew tobacco, play cards, drink beer, and tell off-color stories. Boys seemed especially drawn to smoking. "Clandestinely we smoked a variety of materials . . . dried coffee grounds, bran, dried corn silks, dried leaves," said George MacGinitie. And both boys and girls were fascinated with "bad words." There was an endless, exciting list of taboo words, phrases, and slang. "Bull, boar and stallion were naughty words," Charles Driscoll claimed, because they suggested sex, and according to Lettie Little it was an easy jump from saying "you betya" and "aw, shucks" to drinking and smoking. One bad habit led to another. Parental admonitions to the contrary, youngsters experimented with vices they saw in adults. "Once I stood on the bank of the river and shouted all the bad words I knew, just as loud as I could," confessed Charles Driscoll of his "sin and deviltry."[8]

Children were surrounded by adults who, for better or worse, shaped their experiences and view of the adult world. In the best situations relationships were forged, and a sense of family and neighborhood was created. Children watched, and remembered, how adults came together during times of tragedy and when circumstances demanded cooperative efforts. In Will Cox's Nebraska neighborhood, several families pooled resources to counter the 1863 war-inflated cost of fabric and ready-made clothing. Since most settlers had spinning wheels, they went together and purchased a herd of sheep. Will's father and uncle made a few looms, "and soon most of the citizens were wearing homespun." It was a lesson in community spirit and survival. Juxtaposed beside the need for self-reliance, Westerners valued neighborliness and a willingness to lend a hand. They joined forces to fight prairie fires, build schoolhouses and churches, and bring the occasional recreational diversion into everyone's lives. It was little wonder that as adults, children who grew up in this environment could remember in detail the names and personalities of neighbors as well as specific instances in which they played an important role or lent a special talent to the larger family of community.[9]

Hard Times

The Westering experience brought people together, but it also tested bonds and domestic stability during hard times that came with economic downturns and natural calamities. Difficulties were anticipated, but sometimes the plains environment was more inhospitable than anyone could imagine. Among the most challenging natural phenomena was drought. Dry spells were expected, and plains residents adapted farming methods accordingly. Droughts of any duration, however, brought ruin and deprivation. A drought in 1879 and 1880 in some sections of the plains resulted in failed gardens and crops. "We have about 2,000 people [both black and Caucasian] in our county, and there is not enough [food], all told, raised to support 100 persons," reported one newspaper in western Kansas. Agnes Krom was a child witness to the scarcity of food: "Many times [there was] little or none in the house." Still, her family was luckier than some. "In one home, when their baby girl was born, there was found to be only sorghum seed in the house, which was boiled and eaten by the family. Neighbors took of their [own] scanty supply of food and gave to this needy family."[10]

Land promoters and regional boosters downplayed the impact of drought. With good reason they feared that populations would flee and potential settlers would stay away. In an attempt to offset immediate suffering and halt flight, state and local relief committees organized aid programs. In Kansas alone, approximately four hundred applied for state help when the legislature passed "An Act for the Relief of the Destitute in Western Kansas." Typical among those applying was the Barthalomew family, consisting of Thomas and Lidie (twenty-seven and twenty-eight years old, respectively) and four children ranging in age from one to seven years. A young family without a great deal of personal wealth, the Barthalomews had lost what little crops and stock animals they had. Without money to replace the animals or buy seed for the next planting, the family faced abject destitution and starvation.[11]

Droughts and relief efforts were cyclical. So extreme was the 1886 drought in west Texas that Red Cross founder Clara Barton toured stricken counties while relief was organized, and a three-year drought during the 1890s devastated some plains residents. An Oklahoma girl, whose parents ran a store, saw the economic impact on businesses and "city people" such as music teachers and lawyers, who lost clients when few could afford their services. From the girl's viewpoint, the drought of the late 1800s was worse for town residents than for those living on farms. Who suffered most was a matter of perception and personal experience. George MacGinitie, who titled his autobiography *The Not So Gay Nineties* to reflect his family's situation, would have argued that the rural population had the worst of it. Neither the MacGinities nor their Nebraska neighbors had much to live on, and when the drought continued, there was no money for clothing. As a result, flour and grain sacks were converted into shirts and dresses, and clothing stamped with grain companies' advertising became a common sight.[12]

During some of the most severe droughts, families could ask for assistance from state, county, and private relief efforts. At no time was this aid needed more than in the 1870s, when drought, national depression, and a plague of grasshoppers played havoc with Westerners' lives. In 1874 settlers were just beginning to rebound from a drought that affected some areas and a national depression that wore on just about everyone. In the summer of that year the unbelievable happened: an invasion of grasshoppers, unlike anything seen before, swept from Texas to the Dakotas. A missionary in Dakota Territory likened their descent to "the falling of a snow storm." They covered the ground and filled water containers, leav-

Children and adults are shown burning grasshoppers in this illustration
from *Harper's Weekly*. (Kansas State Historical Society)

ing settlers, including fourteen-year-old Percy Ebbutt, the unenvi-
able daily task of climbing "down the well to clear the hoppers out
to keep them from polluting the water. . . . It was perhaps a little
dangerous, but the well was only forty-five feet deep." Destruction
of crops, stores of grain, and gardens was devastating. It was said
that the hoppers literally ate clothing off people's backs. A terrified
child reportedly asked, "Are they going to eat us up?" Children and
adults fought back. With shovels, axe handles, and anything else at
hand, they beat the hoppers and then either buried them in pits or
raked them into piles to be burned like leaves.[13]

The worst devastation and destitution occurred where the majority of settlers happened to be the newest arrivals with the fewest
resources. Emergency aid programs were established, and donations
of money and supplies arrived from throughout the United States.
In just one month, rations of food and clothing were distributed in
forty-three Nebraska counties. More than nine thousand children
were among the recipients. The aid was welcomed, but many did
not want the grain promised for next year's planting or goods that
tided a family over in the immediate aftermath of the grasshopper

invasion. People simply wanted to leave. A Norwegian recalled that her family left western Nebraska for the eastern part of the state "where they thought they could at least secure enough to eat." The hardest-hit areas lost the most residents. Said a Kansas boy: "They [grasshoppers] cleaned the county of its inhabitants as well as all vegetation. Nearly everyone went back to his wife's folks."[14]

Flight did not end with the grasshopper invasion. A recent arrival in western Kansas in 1886 knew that his family suffered from the current drought, but their situation was nothing compared to the "condition of the refugees who were fleeing." Daily this boy watched them straggle by, and nightly strangers found shelter in the family's home and barn. Since a constant problem for frontier farmers was too little capital, many of those leaving were the ones that had the least. Extended families and emigrant companies attempted to offset the lack of cash by pooling funds, labor, and equipment, but this was not always enough. African Americans at Nicodemus, Kansas, had only three horses in the fall of 1877; by the next spring, all were dead. Without draft animals and no funds to buy proper farming equipment, the settlers cut up sod and planted crops with spades and hoes. Nicodemus residents did not abandon their dreams en masse, but fleeing homesteaders had good reason. Their dark humor told the tale. Signs attached to abandoned shacks and dugouts varied in phrasing, but there was no mistaking the sentiment: "250 feet to water/ 50 miles to fuel/ 6 inches to hell/ God Bless Our Home." Musical ditties, set to the tune of the hymn "Beulah Land," matched the despair. "O! Nebraska land, sweet Nebraska land! As on your burning soil I stand," began one stanza. The refrain picked up in the Dakotas lamented, "We do not live, we only stay; We are too poor to get away"; and Kansans chimed in with, "Oh, Kansas sun, hot Kansas sun/ As to the highest bluff we run/ We look away across the plain/ And wonder if 'twill ever rain." By the 1890s drought severity laid "to rest for all time the idea that rainfall followed the plow."[15]

One has to wonder how the children who stayed under adverse conditions reacted to seeing others leave, or if military and missionary children censured their parents for placing them in sometimes dangerous and often barren situations. Hamlin Garland, both attached to and critical of the plains experience, was sure that his mother was saved from a "premature grave on the barren Dakota plain" when she and her husband were persuaded to leave.[16] The undertone of Garland's denunciation of plains life was not his alone, but it was one thing to condemn the region and quite another to blame parents for the experience.

In the documentary record, youngsters are far more likely to subordinate recriminations against parents for placing them in difficult circumstances and then keeping them there. The reason is both simple and complex. Oral histories and reminiscences are vital in discerning how people thought and behaved, but the essence of these sources rests with narrators who, no matter how unflinchingly honest, consider the actions of parents from an adult viewpoint. Thus the child-turned-adult tends to excuse rather than to accuse, as he or she sympathizes with parents. Martha Gray, for example, spent her first years at military posts on the Upper Missouri beginning in the late 1860s. On the one hand, she tells us that she felt protected. Her parents stood between her and hordes of mosquitoes, childhood fears, and the threat of Indian attack. On the other hand, she confesses that she "carried the fear of Indians deep in my consciousness for a long time after leaving Dakota." She did not blame her parents, who provided a loving home and did their best to reassure her. Lettie Little wrote in much the same vein, supremely confident in her parents' ability to keep the family from going "over the hill to the poorhouse." Little believed that the difficulties her parents faced during their own growing-up years, especially her father who was born in Kansas during its tumultuous territorial period, made them disciplined, determined, and capable of meeting any hardship. Other children shared the sentiment. One young pioneer credited his parents' youth and sense of adventure for seeing the family through tough times, and Charles Driscoll spoke for thousands when he said that although his family lacked many material things, "We never considered ourselves poor people." Rather than regarding themselves as disadvantaged, these youngsters took their cue from adults and adopted an outlook that stressed long-term patience and perseverance.[17]

David Siceloff, living in Oklahoma during the 1890s, realized that any number of things—drought, wind, poor crops, and homesickness—sapped the determination to stay. In his neighborhood, "not a few men loaded their few possessions and families into their wagons and drove away without a backward look or even a good-bye to their neighbors." David was sympathetic, but others were less understanding. In the minds of many, flight represented a glaring flaw in character. A case in point was the woman whose depression after the death of an infant child prompted her husband to send her "back home." The extended family that remained in the Texas Panhandle dismissed the woman. She did not "possess the kind of spiritual timber necessary for a woman to survive the rigors of the frontier." Frailties of women were routinely cited as the cause for a family's failure to remain. It was a viewpoint that not a few Westering women countered by separating themselves from the faint of heart. "The range is no place for clingn' vines," declared a single woman who successfully homesteaded with her sister in South Dakota. "Few have the vim and back-bone to stay long enough to prove up their land under the homestead law," wrote a Kansas woman who intended to stay. Western life was a test of character and temperament. Those who chose to face the test congratulated themselves while denying their own vulnerability. A man who spent his youth in North Dakota summarized it quite simply; there were two types of early settlers—"shirkers and quitters" and "workers and stickers." Western society developed a cultural bias that celebrated the latter, and youngsters adopted a certain pride in themselves and

A well-built soddie (with natural roof) and growing trees add to the picture of success presented by this Nebraska family enjoying home-grown watermelon. *(Solomon D. Butcher Collection, Nebraska State Historical Society)*

their parents for being among those who stuck. Nebraskan George Thompson was typical: "Some of the pioneers with more courage and with a few sacks of corn meal for mush and a cow or two for milk stayed on to share in the more prosperous years to follow. Among those who stayed was the Thompson family."[18]

Strategies were developed for dealing with adversity, but no amount of adaptation convinced some observers that children benefited. "One of the most painful things in the Western States and Territories is the extinction of childhood," wrote Isabella Bird, an Englishwoman journeying through Colorado in 1873. Parental greed and indifference "destroyed family love and life throughout the West." Even when parents showed love and tenderness, said Bird, the struggle to survive stole away childhood innocence. Western life failed to offer the rural environment that was touted as the best place in which to rear children. Instead it allowed children too much independence and exposed them to repugnant, even dangerous, situations. Bird was partly right, but she was an outsider with a decidedly Victorian outlook that failed to note that lost innocence and harsh realities were hardly confined to Western children. Youngsters in Eastern states were robbed of protected childhoods when employed in life-threatening factory and mine work. So too were thousands of urban poor who lived on the streets and begged for their existence. Culturally myopic, Bird was no different from ethnocentric Euro-Americans who looked at the behavior of Native American children and decided that Indians were poor parents. To an outsider unaware of the structured traditions of native peoples, Indian children seemed undisciplined, free to go their own way, and uneducated. Few Euro-Americans saw any relationship between criticisms of childrearing practices among Western settlers and their own condemnation of Native Americans. Nevertheless there were similarities in the way both were described as lax and perceived as deficient.[19]

The innocence of children was of major concern to Bird, as it was to American society in general. By the 1850s it was accepted as basic to a child's nature. After the Civil War, protecting and nurturing childhood innocence became increasingly important as adults felt a loss of personal and national innocence. Untarnished children became the great hope for a better nation and future. Hopes and expectations were translated into a romanticized image of childhood that was unlike any that had previously existed in American culture. In this sense, the Civil War was a dividing line in the history of childhood, not only in terms of defining children's nature but in deciding appropriate growing-up experiences.[20] During the prewar years, commentators might wonder at the advisability of women moving to the frontier, but the emotional impact on children was not discussed, as it was for women. Children traveling across the plains or settling into a prairie home were accepted as part of the westward movement. Without them and their parents, no settlement process could take place. Parents voiced concerns for safety and worried that children were deprived of material things, but staying together as a family was more important than keeping children behind some imaginary safety barrier in the Eastern states.

After the Civil War, Victorian values emphasized an innocent, worry-free childhood. This was, however, an idealized goal that few families, no matter where they lived, could achieve, and it was one that most parents simply did not have the luxury of pursuing in the West. Only once, for example, did Elizabeth Burt voice doubts about taking her young children to a military post in Montana Territory during the uncertain and potentially dangerous period of Indian-white hostilities. And Lydia Lane recited problems with humor. Living at Fort Clark (Texas) in a "funny Little house" that let in more rain than it kept out, Lane wrote of her newborn daughter: "If that poor child had known how many comforts she was deprived by coming into the world on the Western frontier, she would have been much aggrieved, and, if it were possible, would have yelled louder than she did." Discomforts and risks, after all, were no different than those faced by others. It was more important to be together as a family than to be separated for long periods of time. "I was determined to live with my husband wherever he was," wrote Hattie Durbin, who made an uncomfortable stage trip from Cheyenne to the Dakota gold fields with a babe in arms. With the same resolution, Elizabeth Burt joined her husband in Montana Territory, setting out in an army ambulance with a twelve-year-old "maid," a four-year-old son, and an infant daughter whose bed was "a champagne basket padded on the bottom and sides with cotton."[21]

Breaking the Ties That Bind

The struggle to stay together called for more than conquering challenges of distance. Personal losses, economic setbacks, and natural catastrophes destabilized families and dissolved relationships. This is not to say that cases of spousal and child abuse, divorce, or abandonment were a direct result of plains life, but difficult conditions certainly contributed to a breakdown in marital harmony and warm family togetherness. After the accidental death of a son, a couple abandoned their Kansas claim and moved to a frontier town, but new surroundings did not ease the grief or recriminations. The two went their separate ways. Marriages also disintegrated when women refused to follow in their husbands' quest "to take advantage of new opportunities" somewhere else. And the longer Charles Driscoll's family lived in Kansas, the more the father terrorized wife and children with his temper, which became worse when he drank. Anxiety gnawed at Charles: "When I went to school in the morning, I went unwillingly and in fear that the Old Man would kill Mother while we were all away." Charles and his siblings tried unsuccessfully to identify the cause of their father's behavior and the parents' marital unhappiness. It remained a mystery, though as an adult Charles decided that it had a great deal to do with a gap between the first and second generations of immigrant pioneers. The Driscoll children, born in the United States, considered themselves to be Americans. They had little interest in their father's tales of Ireland and his sufferings there. The mother was less attached to the past and more in tune with her children. Over a period of years the father became increasingly estranged, "destined to remain an alien in this incomprehensible country. . . . He was intelligent enough to know that he was considered an odd one, perhaps even by his own family." Although divorce was forbidden by their religion, the parents broke their marital bonds.[22]

Mari Sandoz, a daughter born of her father's fourth marriage, wrote about divorces in her Nebraska community—those of neighbors and of her father, Old Jules. Disappointed that his sweetheart would not join him in America, the young Jules "married the first woman that would have him." It was a mistake. When the wife refused to build the morning fires or to "catch up his team on cold mornings," Jules left. Describing the scene, Sandoz did more than hint at the violence that percolated and periodically exploded in male-female relationships. "Jules closed her mouth with the flat of his long, muscular hand, dumped their supply of flour and sugar to the old sow and pigs, and loaded his belongings upon the wagon to leave her and Knox County behind him forever." Social and religious mores condemned divorce as a threat to the moral fabric of American life. Nonetheless Jules, his three divorces, and serial marriages were not startling aberrations. Divorce was recognized under civil law, though restrictions, allowances for alimony, and child custody rules varied from state to state.[23]

Divorce laws in the West were described as more generous than those in Eastern states. In both the nineteenth and twentieth centuries, magazines and newspapers discussed the "liberal tradition of pioneer days." There was overall agreement that divorces were easier to obtain in the West for a number of reasons—unstable frontier conditions, a freewheeling Western attitude, and a public disregard for social canons. One twentieth-century writer took a nativist view and blamed the "lax social structures" of immigrants. Implicit in these discussions was a lingering suspicion that Westerners, men and women alike, took advantage of a social climate that allowed them to first flout social and religious dictates and then be rewarded with an easy escape from matrimony. Historians and social commentators generally agreed, then and now, that divorce was easier in the West, but the fact remains that legislatures borrowed language used in statutes from older, more established states. If there were differences between West and East, it was in the flexibility of divorce law application and the frequency with which residents sought relief through the courts.[24]

The availability or liberality of divorce laws did not mean that everyone took advantage of them. Cultural attitudes, religious beliefs, and social and financial ramifications kept many from seeking divorce on one of the grounds available. These generally included bigamy, adultery, impotency, desertion, habitual intoxication that kept a breadwinner from providing for the family, conviction of a felony, and extreme cruelty. In late nineteenth-century Kansas, for example, desertion was the leading grounds for divorce, cited by both men (almost 50 percent) and women (over 40 percent). Cruelty and adultery followed, but percentages were notably different by gender. Men (just over 30 percent) were more likely than women (less than 9 percent) to cite adultery, but women (almost 30 percent) claimed extreme cruelty more often than men (just 7 percent). In her study of divorces in Butte and Helena, Montana, the historian Paula Petrik found that desertion was most often cited, with cruelty and adultery again named much more often than drunkenness, bigamy, or conviction of a felony. Among the couples noted were Tom and Elizabeth Fortune, married five years when he abandoned her and three children, and Charles Cox who announced that he was leaving for Nebraska and taking his son. Sometimes a spouse announced his or her intention to leave. Other times an abandoned spouse received word only afterward, or never at all.[25]

The reasons offered for ending a marriage provide some insight into what courts were ready to accept, and any brief review of census materials illustrates that divorced men and women were sprinkled throughout the general population. The 1880 U.S. Census for two western Nebraska and two western Kansas counties provide one illustration. The western Kansas counties of Lane and Decatur were agricultural with only a handful of rural centers. The Nebraska counties of Cheyenne and Lincoln had agricultural economies supplemented by towns that largely relied on the presence of the railroad and the military for continued growth. One might expect that a somewhat larger and more transient population in the Nebraska counties translated into a higher number of divorced, but there were four divorced males in the Nebraska counties and five in Kansas. Whereabouts of former spouses can only be surmised since the number of divorced males did not correspond to that of divorcees. In Nebraska there were three divorcées, all living in the town of Sidney; in Kansas there was only one. The number of children, sixteen years and under, in these households was minimal (only three). Either marriages had not lasted long enough to produce children or youngsters lived with one parent somewhere else. It might be supposed, for example, that the divorced cattle rancher in his forties and the hardware merchant in his thirties were fathers of absent children.[26]

Families were broken by divorce, but death was far more likely to disrupt a family. When both parents died, children were left to rely on adults who might or might not be kin. This was the status quo in both pre-territorial and territorial periods, since an infrastructure of charities and institutions for dependent children was not created until after the initial settlement phase. Thus orphaned children were a responsibility both for relatives and the larger community. It was to be expected that nonrelatives looked after eight-year-old Joseph Robeson until an uncle could reach Colorado and fetch the boy "home" to Iowa, and it was a natural reaction for neighbors to "adopt" two Kansas children after the parents were "poisoned . . . by eating greens." At the same time few questioned the practice of families taking in children sent west by eastern charities such as the New York Children's Aid Society and the New York Foundling Hospital. Despite the difficulties of plains life, residents proved willing to accept these "unfortunates" who were either orphans or dependent children victimized by urban life. Certainly many families were looking for another set of working hands, but it was just as common for families to treat these children as one of their own. Whatever the motives, "little wanderers" from the East were repeatedly welcomed.[27]

During the latter part of the 1800s, charities and institutions for dependent children were organized and began to step in and assume the role once assigned to local communities. Although a few institutions looked after youngsters of all backgrounds, most were exclusive in some way, accepting children of a specific background or whose fathers were veterans or members of a particular fraternal organization. The Mariadahl Children's Home, opened in 1880 and operated by the Kansas Conference of Evangelical Lutheran Augustana Synod, began with three orphans of Scandinavian descent. Meanwhile the Soldiers' Orphans' Home in Kansas was restricted to veterans' children, and the Masonic Widows and Orphans' Home in Texas was only for a Mason's next of kin. Homes differed in other ways too. Some never intended to provide long-term care. The Texas Children's Home and Aid Society and the North Dakota Children's Home Society, both established in the 1890s as affiliates of the National Children's Home Society, cared for children only as long as it took to place them in foster homes. Other institutions kept youngsters until they reached a specific age, such as fourteen or sixteen. Daily life, personal relationships, and individual experiences often can only be inferred from institutional records and reports, leaving this segment of plains inhabitants a silent but present child population.[28]

Loss of both parents was cataclysmic, but death of one parent was more common. At the age of twelve, Catherine Wiggins lost her father when he suddenly died from apoplexy.

> For me some of the light faded out of the world with him and it has never been quite the same since. . . . Later we endured many privations and went through some hard times, but nothing com-

parable to the grief and suffering of those days. Mother was stunned. . . . We merely existed during that winter of 1886–1887— no money, no place to go either with or without money.[29]

Catherine's experience as a child in a one-parent family was hardly atypical. Although it is a small sampling, a good illustration of children living in families headed by one parent can be found in the 1880 U.S. Census for the Kansas counties of Lane, Sheridan, and Decatur. In those counties there were twelve widows and thirteen widowers heading households with youngsters sixteen years of age or younger. In one household a twenty-five-year-old woman was left alone with an infant son, a three-year-old boy, and a five-year-old daughter. In another there lived a thirty-eight-year-old man and three children, ages one to six years. In all, these twenty-five single-parent households included sixty-five youngsters with an average age of eight years.[30]

Widows and widowers looked to neighbors or nearby family for help or relied on older children for housekeeping and child-care duties. One man, living in Decatur County, had four children, ranging in age from three to fifteen; presumably the oldest looked after the youngest. If widows had older children, they took on additional responsibilities, but in this sample of Kansas counties, the majority of widows were in their twenties. They did not have adolescent sons and daughters able to perform heavy outdoor farming and housework. Nevertheless, of the twelve widows only three moved out of their homes. One woman, with a ten-year-old daughter in tow, became a servant, while the two others, both with young children, moved in with relatives. In a time when it was not unusual to homestead alone, most of these Kansas women remained where they were. They might find it difficult to accomplish outside work such as planting and harvesting crops, but it was possible with the help of neighbors or hired labor. And women found ways to earn additional income by selling farm produce or working as teachers, domestics, dressmakers, or milliners.³¹

The stress of rearing children alone forced men and women to consider a number of options. Left with four young children after his wife's death, Isaac Hanson placed the youngest, three-year-old Billy, with family friends. The boy remained there until rejoining his father at the age of fifteen. Carrie Robbins, widowed within five years of homesteading, returned to family in Illinois with her toddler daughter. When orphanages and child-related charities became more common, single parents turned to them for help. Orphanages traditionally took in children during times of family crises (usually for a small fee), and parents used this avenue to provide temporary care for children or, in some cases, maintain the child for lengthy periods of time. Where institutional homes accepted both the orphans and widows of veterans or fraternal members, women joined their children in the institutional setting. Of course, these sorts of places were not widely available or designed to accommodate large numbers, and some parents saw their choices as limited. In Medicine Bow, Wyoming, a man brought his daughter, eight or nine years old, to a couple that owned a grocery store. "I'll trade you this girl for a sack of flour. My wife died and left me with seven." Realizing that the man was determined to leave the child, they agreed. Said a witness to the transaction: "The girl, blond . . . stood with her hand shading her eyes, and watched him out of sight. She did not cry and she never uttered a word."³²

Men and women often remarried, restoring household stability and reducing the level of adult responsibilities taken on by youngsters. For some, including Texan Claudia Hobbs, a stepparent was a blessing. Claudia and her siblings dearly loved their new mother, but remarriage did not create a happy, intact family for all. Cyrus Hagadone's stepmother forced the twelve-year-old to leave his Nebraska home; he was old enough to find work and support himself.

It was a story that somewhat paralleled Bob Kennon's experience. After the death of Kennon's mother, his Texas pioneer father married a widow with children. Before too long, however, there were quarrels over the children and the couple separated. Kennon bounced from living with his father to his grandmother and then back to his father who had married again. Rather than keeping the family together, this marriage created an irreparable rift. Kennon's sisters refused to put up with another stepmother and went to live with a married sister. Kennon stayed, but not for long. After being badly beaten by stepbrothers, he ran away. "I started south and rode all night. . . . Tired, hungry, and homeless." He was twelve years old.[33]

In popular literature and the public imagination, Western families are pictured as two-parent and nuclear. That was the majority's experience, but it in no way accommodates other childhoods that consisted of one-parent families, children who came into households as strangers, or institutional life. Family experiences were in fact multi-faceted, and children tended to expand the sense of family to accommodate immediate circumstances, community, necessity, opportunity, personal feelings, nonrelations, and kin.

CHAPTER FOUR

Education and School Building

—————

🖋 IN 1887 George and Mary White moved their family to south-western Nebraska. Two schools were operating in the county, but the White homestead was separated from both by the Republican River. At times the White children, a ten-year-old girl and a five-year-old boy, waded across the river to reach school; in winter they occasionally crossed when the river froze; and they tried "makeshift footbridges [that] proved unsafe and unsatisfactory." All in all, the result was a small amount of public education and considerable home schooling. Mary White taught the children "in accordance with my time and resources." There were times that she "held a school book in one hand and wielded a white-wash brush with the other," or "propped a book in front of the wash-tub while I rubbed soiled clothes on the wash-board with both hands. . . . I considered it my duty to teach the children."[1]

Educational opportunities were a nagging concern for parents whose homesteading and town building efforts often placed children in surroundings where few or no schools existed. Access to classroom instruction was hampered by distance to school, natural obstacles, weather, or multiple moves. The parents of Clara and Clarence Ewell considered sending the youngsters to Iowa where they could live with relatives and attend school, but it was finally decided that the family would stay together. As a result, Clara and

Clarence "went to school where ever we happened to be"—Iowa, the Cherokee Strip, Kansas. Schooling for many youngsters was incidental, varying in quality and length of attendance. Perhaps no group knew this better than military dependents living a migratory life where educational opportunities varied widely from post to post. Not until 1881 did the army issue guidelines for dependents' schooling, requiring post commanders to find teachers (usually qualified soldiers) and to educate children of both officers and enlisted men. Before and after the guidelines, however, officers often supplemented post schooling with tutors. In one place an enlisted man tutored Mary Leefe and other children in grammar and mathematics; in another Mary's tutor was a woman from New Jersey, hired by the commanding officer for his children.[2]

The constant teachers in Mary's life as well as the lives of other army dependents were parents. The same could be said for nonmilitary families. In Oklahoma Territory the Campbells hired a live-in teacher for their eight children rather than attempt home education alone. But most parents personally handled the job of teacher. A Kansas girl recalled that her mother set up a sort of schoolroom at home, arranging seats to replicate a classroom and enforcing regular study hours. Another Kansas home, that of Emily Biggs, became a classroom for the Biggs children as well as neighbor children. A flour barrel became a teacher's desk, and the young scholars used boxes, benches, and the kitchen table as desks. "Many of the neighbor children got their first and almost their only schooling from Mrs. Biggs." In Nebraska, Will Cox estimated that at least half the fifty-one students who crowded into Saline County's first school "had never been in a school before," but most, including Cox, "had been instructed in their homes."[3]

Youngsters with limited access to schools, as well as those who attended regularly, spoke of the importance of home and the example set by parents. The son of German immigrants wrote that his parents learned to read and write English, and his mother carefully directed her children as they learned to read. A part of home education revolved around family reading. The experience offered a time for family togetherness, but in the process youngsters were exposed to all sorts of literature that encouraged them to read on their own. A staple was the Bible, and children often memorized verses before they could actually read them. Second to the Bible, especially on the frontier of the early 1800s, were the works of Shakespeare. The combination drew comment from foreign visitors, including German-born Karl Knortz who proclaimed, "There is, assuredly, no other country on earth in which Shakespeare and the Bible are held in such general high esteem as in America."[4]

The types and number of books found in homes were subject to personal taste, parents' educational backgrounds, the value attached to literacy, and financial ability to purchase publications. Among Charles Driscoll's earliest memories was sitting on his mother's lap while she read from what the family called the "Big Book," a volume devoted to great events and people in American history. Although young Charles was "frightened out of my wits of tales of yellow fever, appearance of a comet in the heavens, Battle of Bull Run, or the death of George Washington," the act of being read to made him eager to read on his own. Fifteen-year-old Luna Warner recorded the books that she read to herself and those her mother read aloud to the family. "Mama finished reading *The History of New York. . . .* Ma read *David Copperfield.* It is the best book I ever saw." Luna was partial to the works of Dickens, as was Mary Leefe, who fondly remembered *Barnaby Rudge* and *The Old Curiosity Shop.* Whatever the reading material, Mary was among many to credit much of their education and appreciation of literature to their parents. William Allen White wrote: "It was those nights of reading and to the books that my mother had always about the house that I owe whatever I have of a love for good reading."[5]

Appropriate reading material for children was widely discussed by educators, parents, and ministers. In the early 1800s the Bible and stories with a moral were regarded as most suitable, but by the 1840s stories began to downplay moralizing themes and emphasize entertainment. Included in this new form of juvenile fiction were *The Tinder Box, The Swiss Family Robinson,* and *The American Family Robinson,* which was described as "a strange and stirring adventure of a family lost in the Great Desert of the West." Animals and fairies joined the list of acceptable topics, and after the Civil War, publications for young readers flourished as a distinct literary form. No longer confined to "truly moral tales," subjects broadened to encompass adventure, travel to faraway lands, fairy tales, and biographies that concentrated on the childhoods of great men and women. *Robin Hood* and *Treasure Island,* along with the works of such authors as Horatio Alger, Jr., Louisa May Alcott, and Lewis Carroll, became favorites. Some, including Carroll, made no apologies for failing to teach a lesson, and writers intent on conveying a moral avoided criticisms of being "dull and prosy" by creating entertaining story lines that stimulated the imagination. This was a far cry from an early-nineteenth-century caution that "[for children] excitement in reading is a sort of intellectual intemperance and like bodily intoxication it produces weakness and delirium." By the late 1800s, educational theory no longer warned against early childhood education or make-believe. Rather, it accepted the premise that children could and wanted to learn and be entertained at an early age.[6]

At the same time technology enabled publishers to produce books at lower cost, making them more accessible to a larger segment of the population. Besides books, many youngsters were faithful readers of magazines for young people, and they pored over serial stories and special features found in newspapers. Sam Lewis Doughty informed pen pal Alfred Humphrey in South Dakota that he received *Youth's Companion, Western Rural,* and *St. Nicholas Magazine,* "and like them all very well." The Driscoll children enjoyed

Youth's Companion, and the entire family read local newspapers and spent winter evenings reading through bundles of St. Louis and New York papers provided by friends. Immigrants had a wide choice of newspapers in their native languages, and by the late 1800s a number of newspapers owned by African Americans catered to an established plains audience. On the surface, children's references to borrowing, buying, and reading magazines and newspapers may seem simple recitations. They were, however, signaling the importance that families placed on reading and, in the case of newspapers, staying informed. They were also making distinctions between their households and those like Charley O'Kieffe's where "not a single piece of printed matter," except the Bible, could be found. Charley, in fact, recognized the deficiency, which was partly a result of financial hardship and partly one of isolation. "During our first years in Northwestern Nebraska," he wrote, "we had no books, no magazines, no newspapers. The first paper that came into our home was called *The Hearthstone,* a four-sheeter filled with a hodgepodge of reading matter and get-rich-quick, get-well-safely advertising."[7]

Social Life and Education

Home education extended into the larger community, where parents were pivotal in creating outlets that combined socialization and education. A Kansas girl remembered her mother organizing a Sunday school, a singing school, and then a literary society. Anna Erwin's father taught a "singing school" for children and adults who learned to sing parts and read music by notes and syllables; twelve-year-old Anna, a budding musician, played the organ to accompany the "school." Singing schools and literary meetings were routinely attended by Martha Farnsworth and her two sisters. During January and February 1883, for example, Martha's diary noted five evenings of singing school attendance and three literary meetings. There probably would have been more, but Martha came down with the measles.[8]

These community activities blended education and social life. They allowed children and adults to relate to one another outside the home environment, and, when an area's population represented diverse backgrounds, the activities provided a place for strangers to find common ground. This view was articulated in 1897 by the first president of a literary society in western Oklahoma: "Let us forget everything except that we are all friends and neighbors working together in this society to advance the cultural and educational development of the Timber Creek community." Charley O'Kieffe called his neighborhood's Literary and Debating Society "the crowning touch to our cultural activities," and Will Cox was impressed by local farmers who kept informed and "could make an interesting talk on most any subject." At literaries, both young and old participated in recitations, musical numbers, dialogues, and the occasional spelling bee. Organizers acted as a program committee, finding individuals willing to play an instrument, sing, or give a reading. A Kansas diarist noted several times when he and his siblings performed at the local literary: "Curt spoke the Yankee in Love, Grace The Bridge. . . . I read an essay on character." Although the diarist critiqued one of his presentations as a "miserable job," the experience failed to dampen his enthusiasm for literary meetings. They were a "tremendous time." To ensure an audience, organizers intentionally included youngsters, and children as young as five or six participated in drills such as "Choice of Trades," in which each child was handed a tool or an object representative of a trade or profession and given a verse to recite. "When I am a man a man I'll be, I'll be a doctor if I can and I can," went one recitation.[9]

Some literary meetings were devoted solely to presentations or debate. Others included both. Debate topics might be of a philosophical nature—"Resolved: the fear of punishment has a greater influence over human conduct than does the hope of reward." The esoteric was the exception, however. Most subjects focused on local issues, such as the impact of railroads on the area's economy, or they addressed larger social questions and national policies that ranged from woman suffrage to tariffs to temperance. After the two sides made their arguments, the audience decided the winner. It was a simple format that in practice was anything but sedate. Much like nineteenth-century theater audiences that were likely to "articulate their opinions and feelings vocally and unmistakably" during performances, literary audiences were known to stomp their feet, cheer, or shout down debaters on the merits of their arguments. There was also "an outside chance," recalled one Kansas boy, "that a good fight might develop. . . . Some of the younger element carried brass knucks and dared those of differing opinions to fight it out." The literary society remembered by this boy actually grew in popularity when word got around that one meeting had almost ended in a free-for-all between Civil War veterans, replete in Grand Army of the Republic regalia, and "some young upstarts" who had the temerity to suggest that the pen *was* mightier than the sword. Although fights were not the norm, youngsters early learned that statements should be backed with conviction, if not evidence. Also understood were the consequences of breaching an unwritten code of words. "He's lying" or "that's a lie" were acceptable, said one boy, but "liar was taboo as a direct epithet. . . . In our part of the country, somebody was always shooting somebody else for using that most objectionable term toward him."[10]

Common-School Education

The role of parents in children's education at home and in community functions cannot be overstated, but parents wanted children to have classroom instruction. Homesteading and town building opened areas faster than an infrastructure of religious, secular, and social institutions could follow. Not content to wait for territorial and state governments to implement a working educational system, and unwilling to wait for local referendums to establish tax-supported school districts, plains residents took matters into their own hands.

Before a schoolhouse was built in George MacGinitie's Nebraska neighborhood, "the first year of school was held in Grandma Grant's kitchen, and the second in an unused blacksmith shop with a dirt floor." In Oklahoma Territory, newly arrived Euro-American settlers in the late 1800s appealed to the Cherokee Nation to let white children enroll in its well-established educational system, and in one South Dakota community the first classes were held in a granary. These stories from the last years of the nineteenth century contradict any notions that educational opportunities followed a smooth sequence from the pre-territorial period's Indian missions and frontier outposts to well-organized systems at the close of the 1800s. Uneven settlement patterns and differences between areas, even in the same state, produced vastly dissimilar opportunities. Nonetheless the story of education was tightly linked to residents' determination to provide children with some semblance of a formal education under difficult conditions and sometimes in an environment of indifference.[11]

Writing of his opportunities, Will Cox expressed the belief that at least one of Nebraska's territorial governors ignored local petitions on school matters. "I guess," wrote Cox, "he thought the youngsters in Saline County were only semi-civilized anyway." The impression of a distant, disinterested government was not atypical or misplaced. Territorial governments made provisions for public education, but early legislatures, spurred on by regional boosters, gave considerable attention to establishing colleges and universities that, they believed, would encourage town growth and attract settlers looking for "civilization." In Kansas Territory alone, charters were granted to more than thirty colleges and universities, though some never materialized. The ones that opened, usually under the auspices of Protestant and Catholic groups, copied the private academy model that had existed since colonial times. A fee was paid for a "classical" education that included the study of great literature, languages (usually Latin or Greek), higher mathematics, and sciences. In some instances, students boarded at the school while attending classes. By the last half of the 1800s these institutions played a dual role. They established degreed university programs in the professions, and for younger teenagers they provided instruction preparatory to entering college or, in the case of most girls, joining a social class that expected young women to be accomplished in art, music, and literature.[12]

A number of young people took advantage of these colleges and universities. More than a hundred students attended the Episcopal Female Seminary in Kansas where Ovella Dunn studied art, music, geography, English, Latin, "Mental Philosophy [and] Evidences of Christianity," and in 1879 fourteen-year-old Frank Dean, the son of a minister, joined two older brothers and a sister in preparatory studies at Doane College in Nebraska. "It seemed to me," he said, "that I would dread going to such a large institution. It was the largest building I had seen for years." Although academies and colleges provided the sort of education some parents expected, a small number of families bypassed these new educational institutions and sent their children "back East." Fifteen-year-old John Duncan, the son of a well-to-do Kansas merchant, was sent to Ohio with a seventeen-year-old cousin for advanced studies, and thirteen-year-old Andrew Burt, who had until that time spent his life on the military frontier, was sent to an Eastern school. "To educate him," wrote his mother, "was our first duty." Andrew Burt was not an exceptional case among military dependents of the officer class. Those youngsters were often shipped off to Eastern schools when they reached adolescence. Boys prepared for professions, including military careers, and girls had the frontier polished away at finishing schools and young ladies' academies.[13]

Most families, however, did not have the financial wherewithal to pay for academies and Eastern schools or, for that matter, to consider this type of education necessary. Rural homesteaders and town residents simply wanted schooling that provided basic writing, reading, and mathematical skills as well as general literacy in the English language and American history. It was the sort of common-school education that had been advocated since the late 1700s when a series of essays by Samuel Knox and Samuel Harrison argued that literacy in English and Anglo-American history would create an "American" identity. A national system of common-school education would have a "harmonizing" influence as the dominant culture attempted to assimilate immigrants and acculturate Native Americans, Hispanics, and African Americans. Elements of a classical education might be taught as part of the common-school curriculum, but that depended entirely upon the teacher.[14]

With the diverse populations settling the Great Plains, common-school instruction seemed an appropriate and inexpensive model for education. Nevertheless, schools in some places did not always favor the English-only, secular educational system. More often than not, Mennonites' schools were conducted in German, and colonies of Catholic settlers established parochial schools. Some groups avoided the melting pot ideology of common-school education, fearing loss of tradition and language. Some generalities can be made about immigrant education, but no single experience was definitive. There were traditional forms of education in homogenous immigrant communities. Outside those communities, immigrant and American-born, English-speaking children studied together. Sometimes the combinations were unusual, as when Charley O'Kieffe began school at the age of seven. "I drew as my seatmate one Alexander Gosch, a Bohemian immigrant, aged thirty-four. He was trying hard to learn his ABC's in English, just as I would soon be trying to master Swinton's Second Grade Reader." How well immigrants adapted to the common school experience depended upon personality, the attitudes of teachers and classmates, and parental encouragement. Bohemian children in George MacGinitie's Nebraska school were harassed by nonimmigrant classmates, adding to their anxieties and discomfort. The culture clash of language, behavior, and expectations was overwhelming at times. Annie Stella was "a pretty girl, flaxen-haired, round-faced, innocent, and dismayed by America," wrote the American-born boy who was supposed to shepherd her around. Frightened and knowing little English, the girl cried a great deal and wished she were back in Germany.[15]

In numerous schools, student populations were entirely of immigrant background. School enrollments along Swede Creek (named for the first settlers) in central Kansas, as one example, reflected a diverse population of Swedes, Germans, Bohemians, and Moravians. In just one school district the school census for 1877 listed seventy-seven school-age children, most of whom were either German or Bohemian. Youngsters may have felt more at ease without the pressure of performing in front of American-born, English-speaking children, but language acquisition was more problematic when no one could claim English as his or her native language. Christine Hinderlie's classmates in South Dakota were Norwegian and Russian, and "they [the Russians] could not speak any more English than we could," said Christine. To ease communication between students and between students and teacher, the instructor, a Norwegian, insisted that only English be spoken in the classroom and at recess. Mary Sykora, attending a South Dakota school made up entirely of Bohemian immigrants, remembered much the same. Anyone speaking Czech lost "a certain number of recesses." This total immersion, the "sink or swim" approach, was also meant to offset the non-English heard and spoken at home. "How I managed to read, write, and think in English that first year I do not know," wrote Frances Hiltz, who spoke Czech, began school knowing very little English, and was taught by a teacher whose parents were from Norway.[16]

That she and her classmates did learn to read and write was the whole point of what was generally expected of education. Charley O'Kieffe noted that in his area of western Nebraska, "with its motley population from almost every nation in the world," only a small number of residents "were greatly interested in any form of education beyond thinking that every male, at least, should learn to read and write and cipher a little bit." From today's perspective, O'Kieffe's observation, as well as those of others, suggests that expectations were low, if not apathetic. In some households that was undoubtedly true, but more to the point is the inference that while settlers questioned higher education, they expected common-school curriculum to provide the basics. Settlers were largely unconcerned with an intellectual elite. Their goal was to elevate children above the illiterate. One had to remember, wrote Dwight D. Eisenhower, that American society shared a collective memory of Abraham Lincoln, and "few thought it extraordinary" that a man with little formal education had become president of the United States. "At least west of the Alleghenies," wrote Eisenhower, "the well-educated man was more likely to be a well-read man than a much-schooled man. [Even] thirty years after Lincoln, to write a good clear hand, to spell fairly well, to be able to read fine print and long words, to 'cipher' accurately was still enough to go with native intelligence and a willingness to work hard." The self-educated, the self-made could be found in all walks of life, and the perception of self-improvement was accentuated by up-by-the-bootstraps literature such as that of Horatio Alger, Jr., which celebrated the match of a little education with common sense and perseverance. In Alger's *Bound to Rise*, for example, fourteen-year-old Harry, "about the best scholar in school," left the classroom to help his financially strapped family, but this was not an obstacle to "rising" in the world. The idea clearly mirrored what people said of the American West—anyone, from any background, could rise and prosper.[17]

First Schools

Since formal school organization usually lagged behind settlement, many first schools were "subscription," requiring students to pay from a few cents to one or two dollars per month of attendance. In some locales the community selected someone to conduct a subscription school, but it was common for an individual to simply announce his or her intention to open such a school. Rather than delay classroom instruction until official school districts organized, some settlers, like those in Will Cox's neighborhood, took another route. They built a schoolhouse, found a teacher, and supplied the school as best they could. The teacher's desk was "a homemade affair," and students sat on backless benches. The story was repeated innumerable times. In the African-American settlement of Nicodemus, Kansas, school organization was difficult because "not many of them [settlers] had ever seen the inside of a school room." Still, money was solicited to hire a teacher, a man donated his house for classroom use, and in 1879 a sixteen-year-old teacher with "a good common school education" began classes. "It took a world of courage to attempt to start a school under such disadvantages," said one account. "No working materials. Time allotted entirely too short to accomplish much, and anxious parents expecting great results." Still, the children were in a school, and "all learned something."[18]

Education for African Americans followed a pattern similar to that found in Caucasian communities, and in some rural areas and small towns, black and Caucasian children attended school together. Still, African-American education was beset by the recurring question of segregation. In 1879 the discussion before the school board of Manhattan, Kansas, was whether "colored scholars" should be separated from whites in the same school. It was decided not, but by the mid-1880s the school had been divided into separate classrooms for the two races. In Kansas, as in other areas of the plains, legislative mandates addressed segregation. Kansas, for example, outlawed it and then revised the statute in 1879 (when there was a large influx of southern blacks) to allow segregation at the elementary level in cities with a population of more than fifteen thousand. African Americans migrating to the Southern Plains encountered entrenched segregationist policies that were rooted in early settlers' Southern backgrounds. Settlers joining the rush into Oklahoma found a complicated set of circumstances which included schools for Native Americans only; freedmen and children of mixed Indian-black heritage segregated from Native Americans; and one "white public school" with a mixed population of Caucasians, African Americans, and Indians. In some instances, whites chafed at the idea of integration and financial support of schools for blacks, Hispanics, or Native Americans. It was this environment that led some African Americans to create all-black communities with their own schools, and it was the same environment that attracted Caucasian reformers and religious societies to African-American education. After the Civil War the Freedmen's Bureau and missionary societies set up schools in Texas, and one of the first kindergartens west of the Mississippi opened for black children with the help of a church congregation in Topeka, Kansas. Several communities became centers for church-sponsored academies. Most were short-lived, but the underlying principle was to teach everything from basic literacy to courses preparatory to college enrollment. Although these projects approached African Americans as missionary projects, they improved literacy rates and raised expectations for educational opportunities.[19]

Educational opportunities for African Americans were sometimes provided by missionary groups. Pictured is one such endeavor, the Dunlap Academy and Mission School in Kansas. *(Kansas State Historical Society)*

Teacher and Student Relationships

Diversity and race relations influenced the state of education, but the ultimate goal was publicly funded schools with a state superintendent, county superintendents, and local districts. Within the system, rules were established for teacher certification and education. Teacher qualifications moved from anyone becoming a teacher to would-be teachers passing examinations for certification. Test questions usually related to history, reading, writing, orthography, arithmetic, and geography. There were, however, shortened forms. A

"Wisconsin School Ma'am" newly arrived in Kansas was asked only two questions and required to offer a penmanship sample. Generally, test difficulty was based on the type of certificate being sought, the first grade certificate being of the highest order. In western Nebraska, said Charley O'Kieffe, a first-grade certificate was rare; the second grade rather uncommon; but the test for a third grade certificate could be passed by anyone with "the slightest education." Certificates could be upgraded when applicants passed more difficult tests and gained teaching experience. This in turn made teacher-training institutes, called "normals," an important adjunct to the educational system. At a time when few teachers were college trained, institutes were an easy, accessible way for teachers to educate themselves and improve the quality of their performance.[20]

"Good" teachers were remembered in many ways. Will Cox recalled "an excellent teacher . . . [who] took an active interest in instructing us in reading and in 'speaking pieces' and was the first teacher to interest us in penmanship," and Alfred Humphrey was a little less lonely when he began receiving letters from a pen pal, suggested by a teacher who knew both boys. "Miss French has been telling me about you being out in Dakota where there is no-one to play with, so I thought I would like to write to you," began twelve-year-old Sam Lewis Doughty's first letter. Miss French was mentioned in other letters, but the correspondence was much more a sharing of kid information—the names and antics of pets and farm animals, how to catch a gopher, and an exploding pig's bladder ("Aunty jumped up with her spectacles nearly off . . . she was so scared").[21]

Teachers were an influential presence, and since many schoolhouses seemed to have a revolving door with teachers regularly coming and going, youngsters had the opportunity to compare and evaluate. Emma Pospisil, born in Nebraska of Bohemian immigrant parents, began school at the age of five, but no teacher made a positive impression until Emma was ten years of age. Her testimony vividly spoke to the difference a teacher could make:

> The schoolhouse was transformed into a habitable place. Potted plants and crisp curtains were in the windows and pictures were pinned on the ugly grimy walls. . . . Classes were heard with concern, not indifference such as we had known before. . . . During the noon hour we used to gather around her [teacher] like one big family, from the smallest to the biggest boys and girls. . . .[22]

Of course, not every classroom was a haven of learning, and not every teacher was competent. Catherine Wiggins moved several times, making her an expert of sorts on teachers. In one place there was "the first really good school" she had known since coming to the plains, but in another locale the "miserable excuse [for a teacher] spent nearly as much time between 9 a.m. and 4 p.m. in the billiard hall as in the school room." Worse were teachers who abused their position—and students. John Ise depicted a schoohouse scene in which a teacher used a rubber hose: "Exhausted and panting, her face red and swollen with anger, her hair disheveled and in disarray, she ceased to beat the sobbing boy." In a Nebraska school the teacher boasted of whipping every student, even those who obeyed all the rules, and in another classroom the teacher chalked up offenses, waiting until the end of the week to mete out beatings with a hedge switch. One boy, beaten "unmercifully," finally defended himself with a knife, saying, "If you hit me again, I'll cut you to pieces."[23]

The cruelty evidenced in these illustrations may have been aberrations, but teachers were expected to maintain order. Failure to do so could cost the teacher his or her job. Thus some form of punishment was more the rule than the exception, just as discipline problems were bound to occur. Overcrowding and disparity in student ages were contributing factors, as were fights and grudges that youngsters brought into the classroom. Mary Leefe delighted in "fist brawls," sometimes joining the fray. Charles Driscoll accepted quarrels as part of life: "When I was going to school, this fruit [of the Osage hedge] had but one use. It made a good piece of ammunition to throw at any boy with whom you were not on the best of terms." For many teachers, discipline was a problem because most of the students were siblings or cousins. Usher Burdick thought he would like school because his sister was the teacher, "but she was so strict in discipline that one day weaned me from any notion of attending school for a long time." Classroom dynamics also involved a contradictory set of messages: working at home or for others, youngsters had a degree of freedom that fostered independence, but in the classroom, students were supposed to follow teacher's rules. The transition, or the lack of it, contributed to teacher-student confrontations and disruptive behavior.[24]

Misbehavior came in many forms. In one Nebraska school a boy decided to "try out" a new teacher, but "the teacher didn't do a thing but take the 'bully' by the collar" and throw him across three rows of seats. That "put the fear of satin [sic] into the others too." Rowdiness was often attributed to "older boys," but they were not the only culprits. Martha Summerhayes wrote that children attending school at Fort Niobrara (Nebraska) spent "all their spare time in planning tricks to be played upon poor Delany." The soldier-teacher and those like him were at a disadvantage. Officers' children who frequently misbehaved could be expelled, but children of enlisted men could not. Whether at military installations or in community schools, expulsion was problematic since parents assumed that teachers would deal with troublemakers. In one small Kansas town a minister whose son was among the worst offenders, told the teacher, "Well, if you have to kill him, pick up the pieces so that we can have a funeral."[25]

Just as parents expected children to behave at home and employed various means to enforce rules, they expected an adult to control the classroom. Why parents did not overwhelmingly object when teachers went too far is more complicated. Children may not have carried tales home from school, or parents knew but turned a blind eye, reasoning that any teacher was better than none. Just as important, there was no social or cultural consensus on the use of corporal punishment at school or at home. In fact there was no general agreement on when discipline crossed a line and became abuse. Child-training literature, including Jacob Abbott's *Gentle Measures in the Training of the Young* (1871), urged alternatives to spanking and switching. There was one caveat, however. Under no circumstances should children be bribed for good conduct; bribery with sweets or toys created a "mean, creeping, cowardly" personality. Discussions involving discipline, often referred to as "child government" or "child management," spoke of alternatives to spankings, but not all parents or advisers were quite ready to dismiss "spare the rod, spoil the child." If parents still opted for the rod, they were cautioned to dole out punishment without caprice and with a "you cannot know how much this hurts me" speech.[26]

Since home discipline occurred out of the public eye, it is impossible to know the extent of punishments, frequency, degree of harshness, or its similarity to classroom discipline. It is equally difficult to determine the influence of childrearing literature. Unlike references to abusive teachers, childhood writings and adult reminiscences say little about parental discipline. Mary Leefe mentioned that parents were held responsible and rebuked by commanders when children disobeyed post rules, but she was vague about corrective measures at home. Charles Hanson recorded only one whipping, and that was received at the hands of a farmer for whom he worked. Not one mention of home punishments appeared in Charley O'Kieffe's book of recollections. If his mother, rearing her children alone, was "entirely undemonstrative when it came to showing affection," she was equally restrained when it came to discipline. Frank Dean spoke of no heavy hand. "There were table rules," he wrote, ". . . tacked on the wall of our dining room. If any of us misbehaved we had to get up and read the rules aloud." And when Frank's four-year-old brother Arthur persisted in the habit of holding his breath when angry, there were no loud admonishments. "Father came out of the house, picked him up by his collar and soused him in a rain barrel." Arthur was cured. These stories are not meant to suggest that spankings or switchings never occurred. They did, but the overall impression left by childhood memories suggests that moderation at home accentuated youngsters' shock when teachers turned classroom tyrant. The often harsh circumstances of settlement did not translate into equally harsh physical punishment at home.[27]

The Old Schoolhouse

The first school in a community signaled a devotion to education. Vera Best's first school in Oklahoma was held in a dugout, as was the first school in Smith County, Kansas. Of the latter, a woman wrote: "When stray cattle walked across, as they frequently did, dirt sifted down on the heads of teacher and pupils." A small population base and little money in rural areas could not support large cash outlays for substantial school buildings, but early towns were equally slow to fund construction. In 1864, Lawrence, Kansas, had a population of about three thousand and planned for a state university. Still, there was no schoolhouse for youngsters who instead made do with classes held in a church basement. Clearly first schools seldom contained "luxuries." In one Nebraska school, the teacher's desk was a kitchen table, and each family made and brought seats when their children began school. Bob Kennon's Texas schoolhouse had no blackboards. If students had slates, parents provided them. Generally there was no uniformity in textbooks. Pupils brought whatever they could from home. "There were histories from Illinois, spellers and writing books from Iowa, readers from St. Louis city schools, and even some old blue-backed spellers," said a Kansas teacher employed during the 1880s. Teachers added their own volumes, creating small school libraries. Teacher preferences and community values decided what was appropriate. One teacher might approve of popular magazines such as *Youth's Companion* and a "few books of the right sort" by such authors as Louisa May Alcott; another might lean toward weightier literature such as *Pilgrim's Progress.*[28]

Parents and teachers assumed the responsibility of raising funds to purchase textbooks and school furnishings, using the same kinds of activities that funded church building and ministers' salaries. In Yankton, South Dakota, a group of women raffled quilts and hosted a number of entertainments and suppers to raise about one thousand dollars to build a school. In another South Dakota location the teacher organized a basket social that brought in enough cash to purchase a new dictionary, a teacher's desk, and curtains "to make the room homey." Martha Farnsworth's Kansas school held at least one "necktie festival" a year. (A variation of the box or basket supper where men paid to share a meal with whomever prepared it, men bought the basket and matched the tie inside to the dress of the woman or girl who prepared it.) When she was sixteen, Farnsworth was considered old enough to be more than an onlooker, but she forgot the worthy purpose of the event when the young man who purchased her box was a disappointment. "I had to eat supper with him and didn't *want* to, *one bit*" [original emphasis].[29]

The quality and quantity of schools hinged on several factors, including territorial and state law requirements. North Dakota statutes, for example, required that a school be established when twelve children lived more than two and a half miles from an existing institution; South Dakota law said seven or more living three miles from the closest school; and Montana required ten, although

Students at Prairie Center School in Nebraska pose outside their sod schoolhouse in 1891; three of the girls hold their playground equipment—jump ropes. *(Solomon D. Butcher Collection, Nebraska State Historical Society)*

Montana was an unusual case since one school district might cover a thousand square miles. The number of potential students, the transitory nature of some families, and difficult economic times also influenced the number of schools in an area. Single homesteaders and couples without school-age children were unwilling to support schools until a settled population warranted expenditures, and Catholic populations saw no reason to fund public education if parochial schools did not receive similar support. This produced erratic development of local school systems. A schoolhouse newly opened near Fort Larned (Kansas) in 1878 was "fixed nice," wrote a boy. "They have got a lot of charts and maps. Seats just like the ones we had in Illinois." That school was well under way in 1883 when citizens of Albany, Texas, were just beginning to think of building a schoolhouse. Judging by local editorials, there was opposition. "Let it not be said of us," wrote the newspaper editor, "that in our efforts to accumulate money, we have neglected to provide proper education facilities for our children." James Walter, living along the Kansas-Colorado border, waited still longer. In 1887 there were finally enough settlers in his area to begin a four-month school term.[30]

School attendance and the number of schoolhouses were tied to population mass as well as number and size of towns. In 1870 thinly settled Wyoming and Dakota Territory had only 4 and 34 public schools, respectively. Kansas and Nebraska, however, had 1,663 and 781, respectively. By 1880 the number of public schools in Dakota Territory had risen to 508, and those in Wyoming to 55. The largest increases, however, were in the Central Plains where the number of public schools rose in proportion to child population. Nebraska's enrollments rose from 39 percent of its children in 1870 to 78 percent in 1895, and those in Kansas increased from 47 percent in 1861 to 79 percent in 1894. Public officials as well as Census enumerators counted the number of schools and then categorized them by construction type; in Kansas, for example, 75 percent of all school buildings in 1880 were of frame construction with stone, brick, log, or sod making up the remainder. The data may have surprised plains residents. After all, sod and dugout schoolhouses were symbolic of what could be accomplished with so little, and youngsters attending classes in log structures could make their own claims of learning in places that were rough in amenities.[31]

Certainly not every schoolhouse began as a one-room school, and by the late 1800s noticeable changes in public education and funding made them less likely. High schools also began to appear, following a national trend in secondary education that extended the years of common-school education while also offering core studies that prepared teenagers for their adult lives. High schools offered the preparatory course for students intending to attend college; the normal course for would-be teachers; a commercial course for po-

This end-of-the-century Kansas classroom was racially integrated and "graded" by age. *(Kansas State Historical Society)*

tential office workers and business college enrollees; and home economics, agriculture, and industrial arts courses. Plains states passed
education laws that allowed for a high school in every county,
though Montana and North Dakota did not do so until early in the
twentieth century. For younger students, states accepted the progressive reformers' argument that graded schools were better than
classrooms where students of different ages studied together. (In
many rural districts, graded schools were broadly interpreted; the
"big room" and "little room" separated youngsters by age.) Reformers also busied themselves with lobbying for more stringent school-
term laws and rules for compulsory attendance. By today's
standards these laws seem lenient. In Kansas, for example, the first
compulsory attendance law (1874) applied only to children between
eight and fourteen years of age and required only six consecutive
weeks of attendance. Since there was no provision for truant officers
(and would not be until 1903), there was little enforcement. Legisla-

tures and state agencies throughout the plains laid the foundation for public education, all the while understanding that responsibilities at home, distance to school, and parental attitudes contributed to intermittent school attendance or the decision to end formal education after just a few terms.[32]

Considering the primitive structures that served as first schools, paltry teaching and study materials, and a hundred other obstacles, plains residents did amazingly well in educating children at home, through community activities, and in schools. Youngsters were not, however, passive recipients. Stories of walking or riding miles to school, boarding in town to attend classes, or making do with very little are more than anecdotal. They emphasize the time and effort youngsters were willing to expend, realizing that there were advantages in acquiring an education. As a result, literacy rates compared favorably with those in other parts of the country. Between 1870 and 1900 those in Kansas and Nebraska were among the highest in the nation. Overall the majority of children received at least some classroom instruction in the last half of the nineteenth century and, reflecting general attitudes of the times, felt educated. When Will Cox ended formal schooling while in his early teens, he was in the fifth reader, "had passed cube and square root in Ray's third part Arithmetic, had studied geography three terms," and was "proud to say was considered a good speller."[33]

CHAPTER FIVE

The Work of Children

IN HIS REMINISCENCE *Boy Settler*, David Siceloff provided directions for preparing a family's first home garden on the plains. After a patch of ground was plowed up, "the sod was hacked and chopped to shreds. The shreds were tumbled about, beaten, and shaken. The roots and grass were raked off and beds made." Seeds were planted, and "lo! there was a garden." The labor-intensive work performed by Siceloff, and countless others, was hardly the type envisioned by *Tilton's Journal of Horticulture and Florist's Companion* when it advised mothers in 1869 that "The garden is an almost necessary aid in training your children. A child who never learns manual occupation besides play can have no solidity of character."[1]

Both secular and religious commentators routinely warned parents of the risks they took when children failed to learn the value of work. Coddled children were sure to become dissipated adults who, in their numbers, would harm the common good through a lack of industry. Mothers in particular were expected to guard children from a life of idle uselessness by guiding them through work-related responsibilities that were appropriate to age and ability. Few parents in the West would have argued with the basic premise of children learning a strong work ethic, but at the most practical level, the labor of children played a significant role in the business of home-steading and town building.[2]

In towns and in rural centers, youngsters often worked side-by-side with parents in their places of business or professions. Edward and Will Beck set type as printer's devils in their father's printing office, and Della Knowles, who filled her diary with references to home chores and leisure, recorded an increasing amount of time spent at the post office where her father was postmaster. Fifteen-year-old Lawrence Adams acted as "nurse" during operations performed by his father and another doctor, and, while living in town with an aunt to attend school, Charles Brewster spent evenings and weekends working in her hotel. Other youngsters found employment with nonrelatives. A few became young entrepreneurs. After arriving in the Cherokee Strip, fifteen-year-old Clara Ewell organized a subscription school, holding classes in her father's store and charging pupils fifty cents a month. In other towns youngsters earned money by daily gathering up cows kept by local citizens, and driving the animals to and from a common pasture. Dwight D. Eisenhower and his brothers earned money to buy baseball mitts, footballs, and other desirable sports equipment by selling garden produce: "[Father] allotted each boy a bit of ground out of the land that surrounded our house. Each was privileged to raise any kind of vegetable he chose and to sell them, if possible to the neighbors for a profit. . . . For my plot, I chose to grow sweet corn and cucumbers. I had made inquiries and decided that these were the most popular vegetables." Youngsters living in small towns, like the Eisenhower boys, often did the same sorts of chores as their youthful counterparts on the farm. "Town people," wrote Blanche Beal, "had chores to do much like country people. For behind every house in our neighborhood there was a barn and a chicken house, fruit trees, and a big garden."[3]

Perhaps with the exception of military children who recorded more time at play and school and less time spent at chores, home tasks were a basic component in growing up. Boys and girls performed work that was socially defined by gender, adhering to the era's rigidly defined "spheres" of male and female labor. These tasks played an important role in transmitting socially acceptable behavior patterns and preparing youngsters for adulthood. In the American West, however, divisions were often weakened. There was more freedom, and necessity, for women to work outside the traditional scope of their sphere and, while youngsters were reared to understand social dictates for male and female behavior, everyday chores and responsibilities often contradicted the message of gender-defined work. From personal experience and firsthand observations, Mari Sandoz concluded that "often there was no difference in the work done by the boys and the girls, except that the eldest daughter of a sizable family was often a serious little mother by the time she was six. . . ."4

The number of boys and girls in a family, their ages, and the job at hand suspended gender roles. Children did what was necessary. At twelve years of age, Curtis Norton "sewed carpet rags," and a Texas boy spent hours winding balls of cotton and wool yarn for his mother's knitting. Nebraskan George MacGinitie sat for hours and fanned flies away from his sleeping baby brother. "In all my life," he wrote, "I think I have never had a task so disagreeable. . . . Sometimes I would 'accidentally' waken Henry by brushing his face and when Mother came to get him, I would take out on the dead run for the millpond [and swimming]." For their part, girls sometimes worked outside the rather extensive female arenas of home, garden, and dairy. "Nothing quite equaled" the excitement Lettie Little felt when she went to the field with her father to haul cattle feed, and during cattle roundups, Mary Vaughn and her sister, both of whom "could use a rope when we had to," worked alongside the men. Although American-born settlers tended to fault immigrant girls and women for performing field work, outdoor labor was not indicative

Thousands of children, including these boys in Nebraska, gathered buffalo and cow chips for fuel. *(Kansas Collection, Kenneth Spencer Research Library, University of Kansas Libraries)*

of any specific group. Who did and did not perform gender-specific
work was often decided by necessity rather than by any social or
cultural sensibility to a division of male and female responsibilities.[5]

Male and female roles blurred when both boys and girls worked
in all areas of food production, preservation, and preparation.
While boys might chop wood for fuel—"man's work"—girls were
just as likely to perform the chore. Finding fuel for heating and
cooking was, in fact, an ongoing activity. Where wood was available, it was chopped and stacked for use, but its scarcity in many

areas, as well as the prohibitive cost of coal, forced people to seek alternatives. In many instances, families purchased coal only for winter use, taking what they could from the land the remainder of the time. Cow and buffalo chips were gathered, sometimes by the wagonloads. Charley O'Kieffe recalled that during his family's "first chip harvest" the younger children "had to cover as much ground as possible, gathering up all the chips we could find and loading them in piles." The older boys then loaded the chips in a wagon to be hauled home. Most newcomers were put off by the fuel, but before too long, said one girl, her mother went from gingerly handling chips with gloves to using her bare hands and then going "right on making biscuits, without washing them." German immigrants used a process, evidently brought from the Old Country, that mixed straw with cow dung to form bricks called "dung coal." Men, women, and children gathered chips and the materials needed to make "dung coal." Where there were corn crops, the cobs were gathered for burning. Hay, corn, and sunflower stalks were bundled for the same purpose.[6]

Fuel was needed for home heat, but on a day-to-day basis, food preparation demanded a constant supply. Cooking over an open fireplace is a popular representation of homesteading, but when the first substantial waves of settlers arrived in mid-century, cast-iron stoves were making fireplace cooking a thing of the past. Rather than stoop down or lean over open fires, women and children, the youngest sometimes standing on a stool or box, stood over a stovetop or bent to reach the oven. By the end of the century even the most primitive homes had cookstoves with telltale stovepipes marking rooflines. Writing from her "far western home," a Kansas woman announced, "This morning I sawed a new stove-pipe hole through the roof [of the dugout] and put up a tin to run the pipe out through." Percy Ebbutt did not elaborate on the details of who did the cooking in his all-male household, but he noted the means: "We had an iron stove for cooking in one corner, with the flue running through the top." Children, especially girls, became adept at cooking on these stoves (learning to control the heat was crucial), and both boys and girls helped gather and replenish the fuel supply. They carried out ashes, cleaned the stove, and took charge of hauling the water used for cooking as well as cleaning and laundry.[7]

Preparing and finding food was a constant concern, especially during the period when newly planted gardens had not yet produced and, more critically, when gardens failed. One of Agnes Krom's strongest memories of growing up in western Kansas was the scarcity of food, and a boy of the 1860s remembered the exquisite taste of his very first apple, sent by relatives in Missouri. Many types of foodstuffs taken for granted in other sections of the country were not necessarily available on the plains. It took time for orchards and vineyards to develop, and gardens, especially in western portions of the plains, would not support all the vegetables one might expect. Soil quality and moisture amounts determined success, but where other vegetables failed, melons and squashes and potatoes seemed to thrive. A South Dakota girl called her family's potato crop "magnificent specimens." Fields of vegetables were cultivated, and many varieties could be found in the wild. George MacGinitie and friends "would go to the prairie and hunt for Indian turnips," a tuber-like root with a heavy skin that could be peeled away. "Actually," recalled George, "it was rather tough and tasteless." Piemelon (a type of squash) bewildered new arrivals, but through the exchange of information and experimental cooking, housewives devised ways to add this and other foods to the family diet. Some families, observed David Siceloff, did not even try to plant gardens at first. Instead they depended on what could be found in nature. Sheep sorrel was made into "rhubarb" pies, and wild green grapes became "gooseberry" pies. Wild onions, lamb's-quarter, wild mustard, and pokeroot were gathered and used in a variety of ways.[8]

Most often the food gatherers were children. They searched out

wild plums, grapes, chokeberries, blackberries, pawpaws, and per-
simmons for preserves, jellies, and pie fillings. They gathered
wild greens, which Charley O'Kieffe simply called "vegetables out
of place." On their outdoor excursions, George and Wilbur
MacGinitie, "always ready to try anything that had a suggestion of
food value," vied with other boys to see who could eat the biggest
mouthful of the sour-tasting sheep sorrel—without making a face.
Will Cox, his brothers, and their friends gathered walnuts, which
provided an element of fun when it came time for shelling. After
collecting a "liberal" supply into mounds, the boys went "after them
with clubs" to break the hulls, or the boys trampled off hulls "with
our cow-hide boots." In the all-important activities of adding to the
larder and supplementing family diet, youngsters learned a great
deal about flora of the plains. They were adept at identifying useful
plants and avoiding others. At the same time they found ways to
turn work into play. This was evident in gathering expeditions and
obvious when youngsters went fishing or hunting. Both were considered more recreational than onerous tasks, with boys more likely
than girls to engage in hunting. "I was pretty excited over the first
deer I ever killed," recalled Harvey Benson, whose father taught the
eight-year-old to shoot and then "turned him loose" with his gun.
Large and small game, including wild turkeys, squirrels, and
jackrabbits, were standard fare.[9]

The most enjoyable food-related jobs were those that allowed
youngsters freedom to roam. Closer to home, tasks ranged from
seasonal food preservation to daily meal preparation as well as
garden work. Chores were monotonous in their repetition or physically demanding in their completion. The Mayer children, Germans from Russia living in Dakota Territory, spent untold hours
stomping down cabbage in barrels to make sauerkraut, and the
Driscoll children in Kansas were largely responsible for the family's
potato crop. The youngsters walked barefoot through the furrows

Youngsters, like these working in a potato field, spent considerable time in gardening, gathering food, and food preparation. *(Kansas State Historical Society)*

planting potato seed; hoed the field; knocked pests into buckets and then burned the insects in mounds; and after the crop was harvested, spent many winter evenings in the cellar cutting potato seed for the next year's planting. Of the whole process, Charles Driscoll wrote: "We boys hated the potato crops more than any other thing on the farm." Personal experiences and inclinations influenced youngsters' attitudes toward their assigned chores. Blanche Beal liked to pick peas and beans from the garden, but she, like the Driscolls, "hated the chore of picking off potato bugs." Blanche's brothers thought planting a garden was fun because they worked side-by-side with their father. It was far less enjoyable to hoe and weed without his company.[10] Tedious repetition turned youngsters against some permanent responsibilities. Said Blanche of her older brother Carl:

[He] wasn't lazy. He and his friend Frank McKibben, the preacher's son, would work like beavers building their tree house in the mulberry tree. He even said he didn't mind the now-and-then chores, like helping Mama with the chickens. But he did hate the regular chores, like cleaning out the stable every day of the world.[11]

Among the more despised regular chores was butter making. From the time they were five or six years of age, youngsters milked cows, but the job did not end there. The milk was put aside, allowing the cream to rise, and then the cream was skimmed away for churning. Women or older girls generally skimmed the cream, but butter making was a job for everyone. All the Driscoll children, boys and girls alike, had to take "a turn at working the churn dash up and down." It was a job that David Siceloff remembered with intense dislike. "What a job! That churn! The man who invented that instrument of torture must have been an ogre and hated children." Once the butter was made, it was wrapped in wet cloths. What was not set aside for family use was sold or bartered. Siceloff carried butter nine miles to be traded at a country store for goods that could not be produced on the Oklahoma claim. This was not an unusual practice, since rural families routinely sold or bartered eggs, poultry, and butter for salt, sugar, coffee, and sometimes canned goods. Although the term "egg and butter money" suggested small amounts of loose change, agricultural census data and personal accounts provide a different picture. Hundreds of eggs and pounds of butter translated into hundreds of dollars a year. Butter making alone was a home industry that engaged women and children in the production and sale of a commodity that boosted buying or trading power. The Harrington family, which included five children, "met the greater part of their living expenses" with the sale of butter, and Charles Driscoll's father never asked what was sold or how much was earned. He was content to know that butter making "seemed to run the machinery of the household," leaving fewer bills to pay.[12]

The idea of being established on the land or in towns presumes that as time went on, chores became easier with improved technology and families' financial ability to add conveniences. The basic premise is true, though there were wide differences in what individual families adopted from changing technology. Many rural families, for example, purchased new farm equipment before adding up-to-date household conveniences. Changes often came slowly for both town and farm residents. As a result, the steps needed to raise a garden, cook, make butter, or complete seasonal tasks such as butchering and food preservation altered very little. "Settled" children performed the same chores, and often in the same ways, as did the first pioneers in an area.

Herding

Among the jobs often assigned to youngsters was that of looking after livestock. In towns and on farms, children fed chickens, milked cows, or cleaned out chicken houses and horse stalls. In the rural environment, youngsters had the added responsibility of herding sheep and cattle. Texan Bob Kennon set out each day to bring cows in from the pasture (his legs wrapped with cloth as protection against stinging nettles in the fields), and at the age of ten Nebraskan Charles Hanson began to hire out as a herder, earning $3.50 a month. In Dakota Territory the Mayer family had a standing rule. Each youngster had to herd cattle until he or she reached the age of twenty-one. It was no easy task, considering that "there were no fences and the grass was taller than the average man." The Mayers learned to find the highest ground to see where they were and not get lost. Herders also had to deal with the solitary nature of the job. "I think the most lonesome time I had," wrote Frank Dean, "was when I herded sheep for Mr. Baldwin. . . . I was eleven years old, and to be out all day seeing nothing but prairie and sheep was enough to make a boy lonesome."[13]

As these recollections suggest, youngsters herded family-owned stock while some took paid jobs with neighbors and ranching outfits. It was a substantial contribution that freed adults to work at other tasks. Tending sheep and cattle was, in fact, of such importance that some Census enumerators made a point of noting youngsters who spent their time herding, whether for pay or as part of family responsibilities. The youngest herder recorded in Lane County, Kansas, during the 1880 U.S. Census, for example, was a seven-year-old boy; the oldest was a fifteen-year-old who herded sheep while his three younger brothers looked after cattle. Among others recorded in that census were "cowboys." There was a four-teen-year-old cowboy in Decatur County, Kansas, and a sixteen-year-old in Cheyenne County, Nebraska. Although the word "cowboy" was not universally used—Census enumerators generally chose terms such as "herder" or "stock tender" for both youngsters and adults—"cowboy" certainly applied to those who hired on with cattlemen and ranchers to ride the range or work at roundups. Thir-teen-year-old Albert DeGering left the Wyoming ranch where his father worked and signed on with another rancher, and although a novice to trail herding, fourteen-year-old Lawrence Johnson joined a twenty-one-day cattle drive. Because of his inexperience he was paid a dollar a day to handle the horses, find and haul water, and keep the cook supplied with fuel. In Texas, William Lewis and his working partner, a "little Negro named Birl who was possibly thir-teen years old," had similar responsibilities on their first roundup. Driven on by a harsh foreman, they dug mesquite roots for fuel, staked the horses, packed and unpacked bedrolls, and filled water

Although too small for his feet to reach the stirrups, this "young cow boy" (dressed in his best for the photograph) was already learning about future responsibilities. *(Kansas Collection, Kenneth Spencer Research Library, University of Kansas Libraries)*

barrels. When all was said and done, William chose to overlook the demanding physical labor and declared his two-month experience "exhilarating." (Birl's reaction was left unrecorded.) Lawrence Johnson was less enthusiastic than William at the end of his employment. "We were in the rain so long," he wrote, "and I had had my boots on for so long that when I got to the ranch and took them off, the skin came off of my feet with them."[14]

In the public mind the word herder conjured up a more benign image than that of the cowboy, who was characterized as hell-raising and gun-toting. Reputations for drinking, womanizing, and gambling overshadowed the difficulties and dangers of cowboys' work, and Western residents were decidedly split in their opinions of those who chose this occupation. Alma Carlson recalled that her mother was afraid of three things when she arrived in Nebraska— Indians, windstorms, and cowboys. Her opinion of the last changed, however, when a group of cowboys welcomed the Carlson family with a housewarming party. "Most cowboys were just like other people," Alma's mother decided. Youngsters would have generally agreed. "Knowing nothing of that side of their character which had been described as 'seamy,'" Mary Leefe saw only the "the fundamental good and worth which was there." And, for many, nothing was quite so exciting as the cowboy image. "I went cowboy to the extent of buying a big silk handkerchief and a wide brim hat with a leather band," recalled a Kansas teenager who wanted to emulate his idea of a cowhand without actually becoming one. Others, however, were drawn to the life. Jesse Durst in Dakota Territory proudly recalled "his first job as a real cowboy" at the age of fourteen, and in Wyoming the family of Charles McGinnis understood that the boy's "heart was with the cowpunchers . . . at an early age he learned to rope and ride horses and wild calves in his father's corral."[15]

Working for Others

In the work world of children and adolescents there was an endless possibility of permutations that placed youngsters in the position of working full- or part-time outside the home. Scott Davis, who became a bit of a wanderer, left his parents' Platte River farm at the age of fifteen to work as a freighter. George MacGinitie, on the other hand, stayed close to home while still finding occasional outside jobs. He "earned my first man's wages at the age of ten," thanks to a relative who hired him to drive a team of horses. DeWitt Clinton Grinell found steady employment among his neighbors. The youngest of seven children, Grinell began keeping a diary in 1867 when he was thirteen. By his own account, he worked alongside his father in the fields, chopped wood, gardened, and occasionally helped his mother in the house. Just as often, however, he hired out: "I drove Mr. Everetts cow for him he gave me 25cts for doing it. . . . I have been down to Mr. Tynes helping sieve wheat to day." As a wage earner, the Kansas pioneer turned over part of his income to his parents, but a portion was kept and spent any way he chose.[16]

Thanks to the high demand for domestic workers, girls found paying work too. Although youngsters did a myriad of chores around the house and some families had outside help for cleaning, laundry, or cooking, the lack of domestic workers was a constant complaint. In the popular press the scarcity of girls and women for this type of employment was a familiar topic. One paper declared, "Women who understand house-work need not be out of employment a day in the West." Some girls, such as Kansan Olive Capper, lived at home but occasionally worked for neighboring families, especially during the busy time of preserving garden produce. Still, there were not enough girls to go around. Out of desperation, one Kansas woman went to the state's governor. Surely the governor could find her a housekeeper, "from twelve to fifteen years old," among the African-American "refugees" arriving in the late 1870s. A number of African Americans did in fact take up domestic work, either to fund homesteading efforts or to support their town households. Immigrant girls did the same, usually turning earnings over to their families "to pay for ploughs and reapers, brood-sows, or steers to fatten." Over time, suggested Willa Cather in *My Ántonia*, the hard cash earned by "hired girls" played a significant part in establishing their families as successful farmers.[17]

While young people such as DeWitt Clinton Grinell and Olive Capper lived at home while earning an outside income, some

Girls worked at home and for employers, providing essential domestic labor. *(Kansas State Historical Society)*

youngsters contributed to their families' financial well-being by leaving home altogether. After the death of their father in 1857, eleven-year-old William Cody and his older sister Julia planned "what he must do to help take care of Mother and the 3 sisters and little Brother Charlie." Cody left home for his first paying job, freighting hay to Fort Leavenworth for fifty cents a day. Other youngsters helped their families by leaving home and working in exchange for room and board. This did not bring in ready cash, but it did relieve poor families of another mouth to feed. It was this consideration that led an ex-Mormon family on its way out of Utah to leave their twelve-year-old daughter Christina with Elizabeth Burt, who saw the arrangement as mutually beneficial. Burt was desperate for a maid, no matter the age, and the family "seemed glad" to place their daughter into her hands.[18]

Demand for more laborers, both male and female, and the growing population of poor and dependent children in Eastern cities, seemed unrelated problems until charities, particularly the New York Children's Aid Society, connected the two in what became the placing-out practice of the orphan trains. Western settlement required a labor force, and "little laborers" from the East could fill that need. The plan that transported thousands of children and teenagers to the plains reflected the complexity of society's response to children who were caught in circumstances beyond their control. On the one hand, relocation was based on humanitarian concern; on the other, it was a calculated scheme to rid cities of their poor by appealing to an area's need for labor. Great Britain, which had for years transported its poor and undesirables, also turned to the American plains in a brief flirtation that nonetheless witnessed twenty-one teenage boys removed from London's Home and Refuge for Destitute Children in 1869 and dispatched to the English colony of Wakefield, Kansas. This was "a new era in the history of emigration," declared a local newspaper, which went on to report the "hearty English welcome" that greeted the new arrivals before they joined the colony as workers.[19]

Westerners accepted relocation plans for a number of reasons. There was the appeal of demonstrating Christian charity as well as the desire to truly welcome a child into a home. At the opposite end of the spectrum, some families took children with no other objective in mind than to have extra help. Reports of treatment were mixed; some youngsters were overworked and malnourished while others were treated as members of the family for whom they worked. Of those transported to the plains, it can be said that they became Westerners under unusual circumstances. Most certainly their childhood experiences were dramatically altered by the act of relocation.

Relocation was a subtext within the overall story of migration, and as such it drew little comment until the end of the century when states began to legislate against the practice. Equally obscure in the work environment of children and adolescents was the legally binding agreement of indenture. Based in English common law and accepted by American jurisprudence, territorial and then state governments allowed indenture through legislative statutes. (The practice continued into the twentieth century, with Kansas the only plains state to continue to endorse indenture after others in the region had abandoned it.) Youngsters might be indentured to learn a trade or craft skill, but, in its broadest application, indenture bound the orphaned, abandoned, and poor to households where they worked for room and board and received some modicum of formal schooling until reaching the age of majority. Some of those placed out by the orphan trains were indentured, and poor families not connected to relocation indentured their children with farmers or tradesmen to relieve their economic burdens and provide for the child. But the most common circumstance for indenture in Western regions occurred when state-supported orphanages and reformatories (which appeared late in the century) engaged in the practice. Indenture minimized "inmate" populations while providing households with needed laborers. The practice had its critics, but the general public was indifferent to institutional policies that were for all intents and purposes "out of sight, out of mind." Public discourse and rhetoric took the position that officials and charities knew their jobs. If there was any outcry, it more often involved citizen demands for additional institutions. In Dallas, for example, a newspaper editor called on state officials to "give Texas the [juvenile] reformatory and it will be the means of saving many a wayward and runaway boy." That "means" would surely involve manual labor within the institution and, possibly, as an indentured worker outside.[20]

Acting Like Adults

The initial stage of homesteading was referred to as a time of "seasoning." Crops and gardens were still in stages of development and seldom supported a family. Anna Erwin was seven years old in 1874 when her family joined other Indiana farmers headed for Kansas. During the homesteaders' first year, none of the migrants had enough crops or gardens to live on, and as winter wore on, Anna's family lived "mostly on parched corn" and rabbits. Settlers like the Erwins needed money to tide them over during winter months and to pay for much-needed items such as crop seed, medicines, flour, and feed for livestock. A few settlers earned extra money by selling fur pelts and buffalo hides they trapped and hunted, but this became less lucrative as buffalo and other wildlife became scarce in areas being settled. Large numbers of people turned to the collection and sale of what was left of the buffalo—the bones. These were highly desirable for making buttons, corset and button hooks, and fertilizer. Although one frontier wit called buffalo bones "Kansas wheat," collecting them was hardly limited to Kansas. A Nebraska homesteader noted that "many of the settlers make their living now by picking up buffalo bones, hauling them to Kearney, and selling them at six dollars per ton. I and my brothers have gathered a load." Men women, and children participated. John Talcott Norton's 1878 diary included the entries: "We have sold some bones once and have started to get some more. . . . Pa, Curt and I took the bones to town today. We had 1710 lbs., a big load." And in the Nebraska Sandhills, Charley O'Kieffe's family went collecting when it was learned that a man was offering nine dollars a ton for "any kind of bones: buffalo, steer, wolf, even human bones." Some families spent days, even weeks, out on the prairies accumulating a "payload." Others found an ample supply closer to home. "There were so many bones on the prairie the children easily gathered wagon-loads," recalled one Kansas girl.[21]

In the search for hard cash, fathers and older sons were sometimes forced to seek employment away from home. Skilled stonemasons, harness makers, and blacksmiths could find work—but not always near home and family. There was also money to be made in freighting, working as harvest hands, or taking jobs in a town or with a railroad company. Absence of fathers and older male relatives meant that homesteading women and children were left to look after crops and livestock. A newspaper in northwestern Kansas called Bella Blume "one of the bravest little women that ever settled in this great Commonwealth" because she and her children lived alone for months while her husband worked elsewhere "for bread and meat to sustain his little family." When Joshua Wheatcroft's father and older brother left Kansas to freight goods between mining camps in Colorado, the thirteen-year-old and his sixteen-year-old brother stayed on the family's claim, broke thirty-six acres of sod, and planted cane that could be used for animal feed. Another thirteen-year-old, Arthur Adams, was left with a brother to keep the homestead going in the absence of their father who earned money in town as a harness maker. "Both boys grew up feeling the weight of that responsibility," recalled a relative.[22]

Girls were affected by fathers being away, but absence of mothers placed them in adult positions. When the Beal parents planned a trip that involved family business, they hired a woman to stay with the children and put their oldest daughter Ethel, "a month short of being fifteen," in charge of the house. "She could manage meals and chores almost as well as Mama. But she couldn't manage us [four younger siblings]," recalled a sister with amusement. "And the lady who was staying with us couldn't manage Ethel. I think she left before Mama came home." Ethel's stint as housekeeper and temporary parent was mercifully short, but for many girls the absence or incapacitation of mothers forced them to become primary caretakers of home and younger children. An eleven-year-old German immigrant, whose mother was described as a woman driven "crazy" by the plains, was housekeeper and mother for three younger siblings. Cooking, preserving food, cleaning, and child care became the full-time occupation for many who were not yet trained or emotionally prepared. When Lettie Little's mother remained weak and ill after giving birth, it became clear that the eight-year-old, along with her ten-year-old sister, had to take over. "That winter we matured.... Dolls were laid aside.... I'll confess it hurt sometimes, but if Nellie could do it I could too." Christine Hinderlie, whose mother died less than a month after arriving in South Dakota, summed up the feelings of many: "It seemed as if all fun was taken out of life."[23]

Absence or incapacitation of a parent pushed youngsters into long-term adult roles. In the short term, youngsters whose parents were nearby and able-bodied accomplished much of their work without direct adult supervision. An early Texas settler, William Zuber, routinely made a round-trip of forty miles, alone, to have corn ground at a mill, and "sometimes half a dozen boys, some residing thirty miles distant, would be waiting . . . to have their grist ground." A Nebraska boy rode to fetch cows from the pasture and ran errands "several miles form home at the age of 8 or 9," and by the time he was sixteen, Gregory Lacey had complete charge of the family's South Dakota farm. His father "permitted the boy to take over and farm in the new country as he thought best." Youngsters either worked alone or with siblings herding, gathering food, gardening, and in innumerable other chores. Until the Siceloff family could dig a well, the boys—David, Labe, and John—hauled water from the closest supply. "We began filling the barrels," recalled David. "I had a gallon pail, Labe a larger one. John, the oldest, . . . emptied the buckets as we carried them up the bank and handed them up to him." John took the role of adult-in-charge, responsible for both his brothers' safety and completing the assigned task.[24]

Youngsters learned cooperation and the mechanical processes of crop planting and harvesting by working with adults. *(Kansas State Historical Society)*

Given the circumstances, it is little wonder that work experiences resonated with a sense of independence and self-reliance. Entrusted with specific responsibilities, youngsters worked alongside adults or were sent off to do their jobs, either alone or in the company of their peers. When performing tasks without the immediate aid or advice of adults, youngsters had to respond to unforeseen circumstances and make on-the-spot decisions. For some commentators, this seemed a terrible distortion of childhood. After all, American society's idealized childhood contained a work element that envisioned graduated tasks, compatible to age and gender, with the happy outcome of learning responsibility and male-female roles.[25]

At times the labor of children exceeded the bounds of what was considered appropriate by that element of white middle-class America that attempted to set the tone for all society. Girls did the work of boys, and vice versa. Youngsters sometimes worked at chores that were too heavy or demanding for their age, and there is no question that work-related accidents and deaths occurred. Still, homesteading and town building required the labor of children and adolescents. If the country was to be "built up," youngsters were essential participants. For their part, young workers seemed to understand their importance. Many expressed pride, especially when recalling the first time they accomplished a specific task or received pay for a job. They learned self-motivation and developed faith in their own abilities to meet a challenge. These were crucial if one was to face life on the plains successfully. In the process of growing up with work to do and responsibilities to meet, children often made the difference in a family's economic survival. Without doubt they played an active, critical part in Western development.[26]

CHAPTER SIX

Play and Leisure

❧ WHEN NOT HERDING CATTLE or helping with the crops on the family's Kansas claim, thirteen-year-old John Norton and his brothers spent time scavenging for unspent bullets at nearby Fort Larned. "I have lots of cartridge shells that I found where the soldiers had been shooting at the target," he reported in his diary. On other forays John found "two pieces of petrified wood," an old canteen, and a colonel's badge in the fort's trash pile. Younger brother Curtis found a "zinc collar pad" and a bugler's badge. The main objective was finding bullets, but the boys enjoyed the thrill of exploring and making their discoveries. In Nebraska the Dean children (seven boys and one girl) made another kind of discovery while the parents were away. Accidentally they learned the versatility of muskmelon rind: "It slipped so nicely that we all put rinds on the floor inside down, a rind on each foot, and skated all over the floor."[1]

Youngsters played when they found the chance, and they created playthings from whatever was at hand. Through exploration and discovery, children and adolescents arriving in a new place tested the surroundings and satisfied their curiosities through play. Those born on the plains did the same, slowly expanding their explorations from the early childhood confines of home to a larger outside world. Town children found opportunities for fun in the countryside beyond the built environment of neighborhoods and downtowns, and rural youngsters occasionally discovered sources of entertainment in town. Quite often children's concept of fun and play were at odds with adult tendencies to label some play as mischief, as well as adult definitions for what was or was not a toy. Children made no such distinctions. They collected and played with objects that were not toys as defined by popular culture. Clara and Clarence Ewell in Oklahoma counted rocks, shells, and broken dishes among their playthings, and Nebraskan George MacGinitie turned an old broomstick into a gun. Small animals became playtime objects too. Clara Ewell sometimes "caught a turtle or lizard for a live companion," and Bob Kennon had a pet prairie dog—at least until the animal dug up his grandmother's yard and "she took her old shotgun and riddled him." George and Wilbur MacGinitie captured two young badgers and entertained themselves by making "little harnesses for them," and Percy Ebbutt bored two holes through the shell of a turtle, ran wire hoops through, and attached a small homemade "sledge" with a string. "I used to amuse myself by getting him. . . . to pull a little load of wood or anything else I put upon it."[2]

To adults these objects were more trash than treasured playthings, more pets than toys. For many parents, rocks or scavenged trinkets may have been painful reminders of just how little the family could afford in terms of material goods. Children and adults looked at things differently. Objects had fixed meanings for adults, but for children the odd bit of army throwaway or a broken piece of china could be transformed through imagination. Too, children and adolescents spoke of the outright fun they had when making something out of scraps and leftovers. At the age of eight, David Siceloff decided that he needed a covered wagon and built his own, using a box that once held axle grease. He made a bow and used some old fabric for a wagon cover. It did not matter that he had little time actually to play with the wagon. The making was really more fun.[3]

David's wagon was decidedly a "toy," representing the distinct category of homemade items that were fashioned by both adults and children. Dolls were constructed out of cornhusks and cloth, and building blocks, guns, and toy soldiers were made from wood. At Fort C. F. Smith in Montana Territory, the commanding officer had the post carpenter make three sleds: one for the officer's son, one for the baker's three little girls, and one for the daughter of the Indian mail carrier. Baseballs were made by unraveling woolen socks, wrapping the material around a piece of leather or the sole of an old shoe, and then covering the "ball" with a piece of leather. George Thompson received such a ball, made by an older sister the Christmas after the grasshopper plagues of the 1870s wiped out the family's finances. "No Christmas since," he wrote, "with all its variety of presents no matter how valuable, has ever given me the joy and happiness of that little ball."[4]

Homemade toys were produced for a variety of reasons: the sentimental, personal touch of making something for a loved one; the skills children learned when making an item; lack of money to purchase manufactured goods; and isolation from trading centers. In the post–Civil War era, children were more acutely aware of differences between homemade and store-bought as manufactured items became increasingly prevalent and available. A growing toy industry as well as mail-order businesses created a material culture of playthings and advertising strategies to sell them. The middle class literally bought into this culture as a way to reflect purchasing power and status. Things that once were available only to the rich were, thanks to mass production, now affordable for a larger portion of the population. This was reflected in all sorts of play objects, from mechanical toys to rocking horses to wicker doll furniture. One of the few store-bought items owned by George MacGinitie was a clear glass marble with a silver rooster in the center. "I carried this marble around by the hour, marveling at its structure and thrilled by its beauty." He did not say if he valued the marble more than

Doll play encouraged social messages of domesticity and motherhood.
(Kansas State Historical Society)

homemade baseballs or his wooden gun, and it is quite possible that he, like other children, rated toys on the basis of the pleasure they gave rather than monetary value. Social bias, however, more often considered manufactured superior to homemade.[5]

Among the most common items in the realm of manufactured toys was the doll. One historian has called this a "conspicuous doll culture," encouraged by mass marketing, industrial production, and children's literature. Doll play, with its attendant tea parties and dollhouses, was encouraged for its role in social training; but, much like the literature of the late 1800s, it also inspired an acceptable amount of fantasy and make-believe. Certainly girls were the most engaged in doll play, but boys played with dolls until they reached adolescence. This explains why no one in the MacGinitie household thought it unusual that one of the younger boys made doll clothes for his pet toads, dressed them up, and kept the "doll toads" around the house.[6]

Although there were concerns that too much play and too little work adversely affected children, society recognized distinctive types of play as important for child development and gender socialization. Play offset blurred messages of gender roles that often accompanied the work of children on the plains. Male and female spheres were reinforced through play behavior—quiet and contained for girls, loud and rambunctious for boys. Girls received toys that suggested domesticity while boys were given items such as guns, wagons, and wooden horses to emulate male activities. Although American society increasingly romanticized childhood and encouraged make-believe, a Calvinistic undercurrent emphasized play with a purpose. Women were chiefly responsible for ensuring that playtime was fun with a specific outcome in mind. The cultural mandate was outlined in such popular literature as *Godey's Magazine and Lady's Book*, which in the 1870s began two regular advice-to-mothers features. The first, "Fun for the Fireside," provided ideas for entertaining and instructing children at home; the second, "Home Amusements and Juvenile Department," consisted of puzzles and word games for older children. Socialization and developmental learning began at home, and the "good" mother ensured that at least a portion of playtime contained an element of purposeful direction. Structure and content focused on lessons of cooperation, sharing, and proper gender-specific behavior.[7]

One directed activity was the social visit. This was not casual visiting between farmsteads or ranches, over backyard fences or within a neighborhood. It was a formalized ritual that put play in the context of playing grown-up. Young people, especially girls, were expected to learn the art of visiting or, as one historian described it, "that endless trooping of women to one another's homes for social purposes." Children were encouraged to visit one another with dolls in hand. Older youngsters acted out the social niceties without props, other than occasionally carrying the prescribed calling card to be left when someone was not "at home." Structured social calls might be enjoyable for some, but the underlying purpose was social training in roles and etiquette. Ovella Dunn offered testimony to her experiences in Topeka, Kansas, and the urban, middle-class child was most involved in the ritual. Nonetheless it was not reserved for girls or town residents. Recalled one country boy: "A part of my social training was a system of visiting. I was dressed up in my best, my hair combed and brushed. . . . Then I was told to go make a call upon Mrs. Bulch, Mrs. Stough, or Mrs. Holtke . . . [and they] sent their tortured children to visit Mother."[8]

Play, seemingly a natural part of childhood, offered a fascinating set of contradictions. Children imitated adult behavior and adhered to adult-directed activities through play. They played at being mommies and soldiers, nurses and farmers. Without complaint they engaged in activities designed by adults. At the same time, however, children subordinated adult expectations when they used play to puzzle out fears. This occurred in a number of circumstances, including children's response to confusing messages and strong emotions produced by religious instruction and, certainly, the damnation variety of preaching heard by so many. In one instance a group of children created a game called "Heaven and Hell." A haystack became heaven, ruled over by two boys who played God and Gabriel. A cellar became hell, presided over by the devil, and the rest of the children were sinners facing Judgment Day. "Since each [child] was anxious to experience what hell was like, there were more fit subjects for Hell than Heaven." Youngsters addressed anxieties and questions through this sort of play, and since dolls were a mainstay in children's toys, doll play was commonly used to address death, afterlife, and funerals. Parents generally considered this benign, even cathartic. Childhood memories and testimonies suggest that it was much more. Through this form of play, "ladylike" little girls could express feelings and fantasies that would otherwise be unacceptable, and boys could act out roles such as doctor, minister, and undertaker with a gruesome subtext. Rather than play mother/nurse to ailing dolls, little girls allowed them to die terrible deaths, and sometimes dolls were dismembered, with or without the help of a "doctor" who was more than willing to smash and break. "Doll broken, funeral just for fun," observed one girl, and another's reminiscence recalled, "funerals were especially popular, with Becky [the doll] ever the willing victim."[9]

Youngsters could do and say things through play that were not allowed in other scenarios. They could act out aggression and deal with a sometimes confusing world and its perceived forces of good versus evil, or life and death. The drama might be called "Cowboys and Indians" or "Cops and Robbers." George MacGinitie and his friends called it "Republicans and Democrats," the sides dependent upon "which way your father cast his vote." Youngsters constructed snow forts and chose sides for defense and attack, and both boys and girls, especially those on army posts, played at being soldiers and fighting "wars." Charles Driscoll and his brothers faced good and evil in another way. Living on a farm, the boys saw only the town of Wichita, Kansas, when in the company of their parents. Charles could not help but notice one street where red lights framed windows and doorways were labeled "Miss Emma, Miss Lucy, Miss Nellie. . . ." Charles assumed that the signs were there to help the mailman, but he was corrected by a town boy who explained, with his own limited knowledge, that the street housed "bad women." They sat in front parlors or on porches partially clothed, and worse yet, they habitually pulled up their skirts to show their legs. The town boy made no mention of prostitution, which was probably for the best. Charles was already shaken. Bare legs and scantily clad women seemed "a perversion beyond human understanding." Told that the sheriff did nothing to stop this, Charles and his brothers did what the adult world would not. They vented moral outrage and meted out justice one afternoon in "The Hanging of Miss Emma." The boys acted as judge, jury, and executioner. The part of an unrepentant Emma was played by a baking powder can. After a well-conducted trial, "Miss Emma dangled in midair, at the end of a length of binder twine, a lesson in public morals for all the world to see."[10]

Military dependents, especially those of the officer class, enjoyed all sorts of entertaining diversions. Shown here is an afternoon of croquet at Fort Bridger, Wyoming Territory (ca. 1873). *(National Archives and Records Administration)*

Games and Sports

Children's activities extended into a number of games and physical activities. During winter months there were sleigh rides and ice skating. Wrote John Norton in his diary: "[Brother] Curt went skating on the Sawmill with the skates he traded Homer Kenton his knife for. He broke through and got wet." In the summer youngsters went fishing and swimming. George MacGinitie's sisters and their friends wore dresses "like long nightgowns," the hems weighted with sand to keep the "skirts from floating up." Horseback riding was a constant source of amusement. Youngsters learned to ride at an early age. "Kids in those days," wrote Bob Kennon of his Texas childhood, "were raised in the saddle." Riding was a valued skill and in some social circles a required accomplishment. On horseback, youngsters had freedom to wander and explore.

Kennon described it as being "independent-like . . . as we roamed over the prairies." Children and adolescents raced and tried stunts, and military dependents, not engaged in the business of home-steading and town building, found it a primary form of entertainment. Nonmilitary youngsters were often expected to use riding abilities to herd or run errands or get themselves to and from school. Nevertheless horseback riding was one of those instances in which work and fun became indistinguishable, as was hunting, which boys found to be more fun than a chore of gathering food. The Norton brothers shot at rattlesnakes, birds, jackrabbits, and prairie chickens. Sometimes they missed a target, and occasionally they "did not see anything" on tramps across the countryside. For these boys a jackrabbit for dinner was an added prize to an already exciting day of adventure. Dinner was definitely the last thing on James Walker's mind. At the age of nine he was handling "an old muzzle loading shot gun," and by the age of ten he and his friend George were hunting the environs outside Fort Berthold with a Winchester "pump gun." "One time," wrote James, "we brought home a big, fat badger . . . and we had no idea what kind of creature we had killed, but whatever it was we were greatly elated."[11]

The impression left by these sorts of accounts is one of spontaneous play that may or may not have had adult supervision. Parental figures might appear only on the sidelines of these stories, or they do not appear at all. As in the world of work, youngsters had freedom, and the possibilities for play were many. Still, parents were a force in children's play, and there is little evidence to suggest that parents expected youngsters to engage in only one type of play. Different forms of play and toys provided varying opportunities for fun, socialization, and the development of physical and mental skills. Another category of play, then, consisted of games with long-standing rules or patterns. Danish youngsters recalled cardplaying as a winter amusement: "Six or eight persons, young and old, would often gather about a table and, with matches as counters, play the

Simple games that required little if any equipment could be played most anywhere, including school playgrounds. *(Kansas State Historical Society)*

game of 'Three-Cards' (*tre-kort*). . . . The younger folks would find great amusement in a game of '*Sort Pe'er*' (Black Peter)." Generally, group games were extremely popular, no matter a child's ethnic, cultural, or racial background. The games were democratic because usually any number and any age could play. Games such as run geese run, blindman's buff, skinny, musical chairs, hide 'n seek, variations of tag, and skip rope could be played most anywhere. The rules were simple, and few if any toys or equipment were required. Even the game of baseball required very little equipment, and often that was homemade. The game was popular at military posts, in towns (which sometimes had their own teams and leagues), and at country schools. Martha Farnsworth happily played at noon recess: "Boys have their '9', and we girls our '9' and when we play against the Boys we beat them every time."[12]

The play of Farnsworth and her friends and antics such as Mary Leefe's "wild kick-up leap" at tennis outraged some, but decorum did not forbid girls from taking part in games that required physical exertion. In fact childrearing literature urged parents to encourage "bodily locomotion," and there was general approval of structured games for both boys and girls. This sort of activity taught cooperation and teamwork. Educators suggested that group games favorably manipulated a child's environment for the public good, and some commentators believed that organized games hastened immigrant assimilation into the dominant culture. There were also progressive reformers who added the argument that structured games deterred juvenile delinquency because youngsters learned to follow rules and subordinate individuality. For children, on the other hand, games were fun, a test of abilities, and a chance to be with peers. Games also offered a quick way for plains children to enter into kid society when they were newcomers or on the move. On one of the Milton family's rest-over stops on the way to Kansas, for example, daughter Jennie wrote, "We had company. A little girl and we jumped rope." Westerners were known for openly greeting strangers and establishing instant intimacies of conversation and shared meals. Children imitated adults in the currency they understood—play.[13]

Adults assigned certain outcomes to structured activities, and saw the results. Nevertheless Western children showed a penchant, even in group activities, to demonstrate the individuality so upsetting to social reformers. The historian Elliott West called this a result of the frontier's "achievement culture," in which children quickly learned that Western society praised individualism and aggressive behavior. The fastest, the strongest, the quickest thinking were applauded while lessons of sportsmanship and cooperation were sometimes lost in the fray. "It [game of croquet] ended with a quarrel. Grace S. hitting Grace E. on the back with a mallet," wrote a Kansas teenager. The cooperative spirit preached by adults did not die in the plains experience. It was simply asked to coexist with individualism. Rather than two opposing ideas, Westerners saw cooperation and individual interest as two necessary sides of life's lessons.[14]

Community Play

Opportunities for fun and social contact came in an assortment of possibilities. Youngsters not only played together, but in the larger community of town or rural neighborhoods they intermingled with adults while enjoying the company of their peers. In this adult-child environment, play parties were common, popular outings. The "playing" consisted of singing a cappella while keeping in step with various movements such as promenading, swinging partners, skipping, or dancing in circles of four to eight people. Familiar tunes were "Weevily Wheat" and "Old Dan Tucker" and "Skip-to-My-Lou." Sometimes old songs were given new verses to reflect Western life. The words to "The Farmer in the Dell" were reworked into "Oh, we'll shoot the Buffalo, Yes, we'll shoot the Buffalo." The only thing that kept a play party from being a "dance" was a fiddle, banjo, or piano. In the eyes of many, the lack of a musical instrument made all the difference in social propriety. As Percy Ebbutt observed, "There were a great many Methodists and others who look upon dancing as an unpardonable sin." Percy and others thought it odd that people who thought "dancing was an invention of the devil" did not object to party games that included kissing. Charles Driscoll's mother drew the line at kissing, only to be overruled by her husband who decided to introduce a game "that we used to play in Ireland." When the leader called a halt to the singing, he shouted out, "All turn around and kiss your partner!" And they did. At issue was not the familiarity of kissing but dancing as an "occasion of sin."[15]

Play parties were prevalent, but some thought they were "only dancing with the best part of it, the music, left out." After all, the point of disapproval was movement set to music, not the music itself. Instrumental music and choral presentations were integral to church services, home entertainment, classroom routines, singing schools, and community activities. Many immigrant settlements formed choral groups that performed at both secular and religious events, and towns pointed with pride to "their" bands. On an individual level, youngsters belonged to choruses and learned to play instruments. DeWitt Clinton Grinell happily joined a brass band when "the Saxophones arrived," and the Beal household reveled in its musical evenings. The father played hymns and "simple tunes" on a fiddle; mother played the piano; the oldest boy, the violin; and the oldest girl, the cello. The two youngest girls sang duets, and "Papa could hardly wait till Carl got through his first lessons on the cornet so he could join in playing part music."[16]

Despite some communities' objections to dancing accompanied by instruments, music and dancing were enjoyed in social gatherings. The waltz, polka, schottische, reel, and square dance were often mentioned in youngsters' accounts. When he was ten years old, George MacGinitie began attending dances held in town, sometimes alone. Martha Farnsworth, on the other hand, danced for the very first time in her life when she was fifteen. The occasion was a "little party" attended by more than thirty people in the family home. Occasionally it was some distance to a dance, and many lasted well into the night. Young people, often unchaperoned, might not make it home until the next day. On snowy winter outings, recalled Will Cox, a wagon box was placed on a pair of bobsleds and "away we would go [to the dance], taking every boy and girl on the route." The memory coincided with the experience of Della Knowles who recorded going off to a party with twelve others in a "lumber wagon." No adults were mentioned in either account.[17]

Residents of towns and more densely populated rural areas had more opportunities for varied entertainment. Towns with just a few hundred in population had an opera house that attracted traveling shows and individual performers. Old favorites and new programs provided entertaining and cultural diversions. Willa Cather recalled the excitement that accompanied the arrival of actors and announced programs for the opera house in Red Cloud, Nebraska: "My playmates and I used to stand for an hour after school, studying every word on those posters; the names of the plays and the nights on which each would be given. . . . How good some of those old traveling companies were, and how honestly they did their work and tried to put on a creditable performance." Writing years after the fact, Cather wanted to convey what the theater meant to her as an eleven-year-old, and chose to highlight uplifting and classical presentations such as an opera company's performance of *The Bohemian Girl* or plays such as *Damon and Pythias*. There were, of course, all sorts of entertainments. A Kansas girl "very much" enjoyed the melodrama *Married for Money*; it was the only production recorded in her one-year diary. As these two girls' experiences suggest, there were "cultural" entertainments and there were the "popular." These labels, however, were much more an invention of the late-nineteenth-century upper class than rigid definitions applied by audiences during most of the 1800s. Certainly some people were more discriminating than others. The content of some entertainments was considered unsuitable for children or genteel women, and religious beliefs kept some from attending the theater but not, as a rule, skits presented in the context of a literary meeting. Nonetheless entertainments were there for the taking, and there was something for everyone—opera, variety vaudeville, comedy, drama, medicine shows, and readings of Shakespeare.[18]

To Cather, nothing quite made an impression like living people on a stage, but Lettie Little, whose family went to town only once a month, "had never known such a thrill" as the late-nineteenth-century moving pictures of a nickelodeon. Children, like adults, enjoyed entertainments that took them out of everyday life, if only for a short time. One of the most fanciful was the circus with its exotic animals, death-defying acts, and colorful costumes. After attending a circus in Valentine, Nebraska, Alma and Emma Carlson decided to imitate the girl stunt riders. "We took ribbons and tied them around our waists making our dresses very short," wrote Alma, "and played riding horses on the rafters in the granary." Mary Leefe and her friends at Fort Ringgold were just as enthusiastic: "We performed all sorts of stunts on a trapeze with bad falls and risky horseback riding of horses."[19]

In the search for diversion and entertainment, people in sparsely settled areas had fewer opportunities. Still, some made considerable efforts to carve out time for play and make their own fun. In one western Kansas community, for example, the local stockman's association held a "Play-Day" that drew about two hundred men, women, and children for a "day of social recreation." Families brought picnic meals, a band played, speeches were made, and a dance "lasted into early morning." On the plains, people made their own fun with community socials as well as those sponsored by women's groups, fraternal organizations, and local school districts. Among immigrant groups, bonds were established and maintained through their "halls" where events—parties, dances, theater performances, and athletic associations—provided much of a community's social life. Just as important were church and Sunday school gatherings. Dwight D. Eisenhower summed up the experience when writing of his small, end-of-the-century community where "social life centered around the churches." He fondly recalled church picnics where "the men pitched horseshoes, the women knitted and talked, the youngsters fished, and everyone recovered from the meal." Picnics, church suppers, and socials produced immediate moments of enjoyment and fond memories.[20]

Celebrating Special Occasions and Holidays

A cornerstone of the social life of families and communities was the celebration of special days. African Americans observed the liberation of slaves in the West Indies through Emancipation Day, and immigrants imported celebrations that ranged from St. Patrick's Day to annual festivals. Some of these celebrations remained closed to outsiders, but by the end of the century many ethnic communities welcomed the general public to celebrations. It was a unique opportunity to reach out and teach outsiders about a group's culture, and some hoped that open invitations would lessen tensions with a temperance-minded society that censured immigrants whose cultures found nothing wrong with making and consuming beer and wine. Certainly prohibitionists were not convinced that groups should maintain these customs, but annual events allowed immigrants to both enjoy their traditions and educate the public at large. Said a newspaper announcing a German day of festivities open to the public, "Anything can be had from good old-fashioned lager beer to a square meal."[21]

Childhood memories recalled particular celebrations and holidays. Some families celebrated birthdays with small gifts or the preparation of a special meal, and immigrants often made a point of remembering the birthdays of relatives back in Denmark or Sweden or Germany as if they were present. Not all families, however, made it a practice to celebrate birthdays. John Talcott Norton's diary entry for October 1, 1877, recorded: "Today is my birthday. I am 14 years of age." During the day he shot at some ducks, caught escaped pigs, and his mother was called to help deliver a baby. There was no mention that his family noted the day. Thirteen-year-old DeWitt Clinton Grinell's birthday was much the same: "Have been hunting and fishing to day this fore noon I worked in the Garden to day is my birth day."[22]

Among other holidays, some families celebrated Thanksgiving, but, again, not every household recognized the day. And, coloring eggs at Easter was only occasionally noted by youngsters in their writings. Independence Day, however, was celebrated almost universally. Daylong observances featured parades, picnics, obligatory political speeches, and orations that reinforced feelings of patriotism and American ideals. Sometimes there were dances or horse races. In territorial Kansas, "juvenile pioneers" in one town paraded down the street to a grove where the children sang amid a "bright display of ribbons and wreaths." At one celebration, DeWitt Clinton Grinell set off plenty of fireworks "and would have had more had not the box containing them accidentally caught fire and burnt up," and a Kansas teenager saved "some baby firecrackers as a relic of the marvelous fourth." Military veterans were a fixture at celebrations. There was always a "contingent of marching Civil War Veterans, many of them dressed in their old uniforms," recalled one Nebraskan. Youngsters living in institutions, where recreational outlets were few, also celebrated the day. A report from the Girls' Training School in Nebraska noted that the eighty-one residents each received "an abundance of firecrackers" before leaving the institution for a picnic: "We all started for a grove on the creek about a mile distant where the day was spent in a most enjoyable manner."[23]

Children and adolescents wrote about a number of holidays and celebrations, but none was mentioned or recalled more often than Christmas. Occasionally, poignant memories recalled the disappointment of no presents and little to celebrate. Other stories spoke of few material goods but happy family celebrations. Vera Best's Oklahoma holidays consisted of "sticks of red candy . . . that was all we had," but Kansan Henry Norton listed much more. "Found a lead pencil, some candy and raisins and a good sized red handkerchief in my stockings." Sisters Lucy and Mary each received a doll, and brother George got a marble game and handmade wooden gun.

In a photograph labeled "Christmas at the Ranch," the Walbridge sisters sit surrounded by the ideal trappings of a Victorian Christmas—a trimmed tree and Santa-delivered toys. *(Kansas Collection, Kenneth Spencer Research Library, University of Kansas Libraries)*

Other than gifts received, or the lack of them, youngsters mentioned Christmas trees, either at home or church or schoolhouse. That would be expected, but a tree takes on additional significance when it is remembered that trees were not readily available in wide expanses of the plains. It took some effort to locate them, and in some instances it took adaptive innovation. "The first Christmas tree I remember was a tumble-weed," wrote a Kansas boy. The tumbleweed "tree" was "decorated with paper chains, some little gifts that Mother had made and pictures of birds and flowers from Arbuckles coffee." The Beal household "never had a tree at home." The family's tradition was to hang stockings filled with presents the children made for one another.[24]

The blend of home celebrations and religious observances left children with a wealth of memories and impressions. Rituals differed according to faith and ethnic customs. In some Swedish families, children left their shoes outside the door to be filled with sweets or small presents, and the first day of the holiday began with the oldest daughter serving coffee and cookies to the household. In some German Russian communities, children dreaded the arrival of St. Nicholas for he went from house to house reprimanding children and withholding candy. Other children enjoyed more festive traditions. In a number of Volga German communities, the *Pelznickel*, a man dressed in heavy coat and wrapped in chains, arrived first, listing children's misdeeds and extracting promises for good behavior. Following him was *Kristkind*, portrayed by a woman dressed in white, who brought gifts and sweets. Catholic and Protestant church services observed the religious meaning of the holiday, and most combined secular practices. At Ovella Dunn's Methodist Sunday school there was a concert followed by the unveiling of a Christmas tree "strewed with Pop Corn & Candy" and enough presents for every child attending. Several Sunday schools in Abilene, Kansas, united to have a Christmas tree, concert, and "the appearance of Santa Claus as big as life and a distribution of gifts." George MacGinitie declared that the "most exciting entertainment [I] ever attended" was the Christmas program held in the new schoolhouse when he was five years old. There was a tree, a program of Christmas songs, and a visit from Santa who handed out bags of candy.[25]

On military posts, pains of separation from family and friends "back home" were soothed by making a special effort to create a season of joy and cheer. Adults derived enjoyment from the festive, memorable time created for children. Even on isolated posts where goods were difficult if not impossible to obtain, there were decorations and gifts. At Fort C. F. Smith, the post tree was decorated with cookies, doughnuts, chains made of colored paper, and paper cornucopias filled with homemade candy. A few families had trees in their quarters, but post Christmas parties brought everyone together in a main hall festooned with garlands and candles. Santa arrived and gifts were distributed. Some toys were store-bought, ordered from far away, but many were made by adults at the post. On "far-off plains posts," officers, enlisted men, women, and children gathered as a large family, continuing traditions and enlivening children's experiences.[26]

Celebrations of special days, whether tied to religious beliefs or secular observances, provided time to play and to enjoy a break from everyday routines. At the same time, observances bound youngsters to community and family as well as to ethnic, religious, and/or racial heritages. Celebrations, recreation, and playtime were not afterthoughts squeezed between work and education. Rather, they were a recognized part of growing up. Youngsters either made their own entertainment or found it with their families and through community activities. They were not deterred by hard times, isolation, or the transient nature of Western culture. Fun was found in chores, tramping across the countryside, and organized games. Youngsters learned adult roles through play, and they discovered individual skills and talents. Children confronted fears and tested themselves against an environment that demanded exploration. Theatrical entertainments, community socials, and special celebrations provided enjoyable experiences that shaped youngsters' ideas about culture and life in the West. The simple play of children was never really that simple.

CHAPTER SEVEN

Matters of Life and Death

❧ "ICE CRACKED ON THE QUILT where leaking rain had fallen. Wind howled around the shanty and from the roof and all the walls came a sound of scouring." On a South Dakota claim the Ingalls family awoke to a freak October blizzard that took everyone by surprise but foretold the hard winter to come. For three days the family waited out the storm that tore away part of the shanty's tarpaper roof. When the blizzard passed, Charles Ingalls hurried the family to prepare for a move to town. Of the coming winter he confided, "If you must have the truth, I'm afraid of it."[1]

He had good reason to be. In a world that offered little protection from life-threatening diseases and accidents, only the foolhardy failed to exercise caution when there was an opportunity to exert some measure of control over possibly dangerous situations. For all of its potential and beauty, the natural environment was not to be trusted. Quick changes in weather, as well as unpredictable prairie fires, could kill. Such events did not take lives in epidemic proportions, but they represented a frightful, even awe-inspiring test of survival. Years after the fact, Joshua Wheatcroft still seemed surprised at surviving a blizzard that caught him while herding cattle: "I was all alone in a little tent out on the wide open prairie, with nothing but the thickness of a canvas between me and eternity." Some blizzards went down in history and local lore as the worst and offered cautionary tales of prudent vigilance. The Easter blizzard of 1873 became a lasting memory for many on the Central Plains. "Those [Bohemian immigrants] that had corn to burn were in luck," recalled one Nebraskan, "but many burned their furniture to cook their meals and keep their families from freezing." Facing the same storm, the Dean family was just approaching its first anniversary of Nebraska settlement. Ten-year-old Frank Dean remembered the danger of not being able to see two hundred feet from the back door. His brother Horace, who was fifteen, tied a rope around his waist before going out to tend the livestock. The rope was let out from the house, and said Frank, "It was fortunate Horace did have the rope, for he made three attempts before he found the stables."[2]

Then there was the great "die-up" of 1886. "Just before the storm broke the weather was mild and still. . . . I can remember so well as we were playing out-of-doors," recalled a boy on the Kansas prairie, where nothing obstructed his view of a heavy cloud bank that swept before it hundreds of birds "traveling with all the speed they possessed to get out of the path of the storm." During the blizzard that followed, thousands of cattle died, people caught outdoors perished, and those with shelter wondered if they would survive. "It lasted so long," recalled one Kansan, "that Dad was on the point of tearing up the board floor and burning it for fuel." The parents protected an infant son by wrapping him in blankets and setting him "on the oven door." After the storm, homesteaders searched "dugouts, shanties and prairie . . . [and] a number of people were found in their homes frozen to death."[3] Among them was a family of seven:

> Upon finding them it was discovered that they had burned up all their fuel, and also the furniture; and after that was gone, having no place to resort to without exposure to the severity of the elements then prevailing, they all retired to bed in hopes of keeping

warm . . . until relief could be obtained, but none came save through death.[4]

Historically the blizzard of 1886 receives more attention for its devastating effect on the cattle industry than for its human toll, but one blizzard, that of 1888, is remembered as the "schoolchildren's storm." It was a tragedy that drew national attention. New York–based *Frank Leslie's Illustrated Newspaper* reported that plains residents, from Texas to Montana, suffered from the intense cold, but the saddest stories were those of child victims. The storm hit just when children were on their way home from school or about to leave. A Swedish immigrant recorded the day in his diary, unable to do anything but wait out the storm: "We are much worried over the children. . . . I have gone halfway but dared not go further as [I] feared for my life. We hope the children stayed in the schoolhouse and the teacher with them. . . . Now we must go to bed and leave all in God's hands." (The next day he found the children safe.) Some teachers became heroes for making decisions that saved students' lives. As the wind blew out schoolhouse windows and then collapsed the roof, nineteen-year-old Minnie Mae Freeman bound "thirteen little scholars" to her with twine and led them to a safe house about a mile away. Freeman was, said a newspaper, the "brave heroine of the blizzard." Unfortunately, others made the wrong choices and perished. A teacher and a little girl died together on the prairie, the child wrapped in the teacher's skirts. Four children froze to death in a schoolhouse, left there by a teacher who went for help, and another teacher, with nine children, abandoned the schoolhouse—but without any sort of lifeline. Blinding snow and howling wind quickly separated the group, and it took days to find the scattered bodies.[5]

Blizzards were dramatic reminders of settlers' fragile existence in the face of natural forces. So too were prairie fires that both mesmerized and terrified. Ovella Dunn wrote of the beauty of a prairie fire at night, while an Oklahoma girl knew the terror of fire racing through "grass as high as a man's head." William Allen White remembered the thrill that he and classmates felt when they returned to school as "tired boy heroes" ready to boast of their fire-fighting exploits. While men plowed fireguards, women and children beat back flames with wet gunnysacks. Bertie Canfield and his siblings joined with adults to protect his house and outbuildings successfully from a fire that was "coming this way quite fast," and fourteen-year-old Frank Dean, left at home while the rest of the family was away, managed to contain a blaze until help arrived. He had nothing but his water-soaked coat and quick thinking "to fight the fire down." One of George MacGinitie's classmates became "something of a hero" because he saved himself from a fast-moving fire by driving horse and cart "on a run directly into and through the approaching fire." Others were not so lucky. As a fire swept toward a Nebraska schoolhouse, a mother ignored teacher protests and retrieved several children. The fire overtook the woman and the ten children with her; their bodies were later found "scattered over a blackened, smoldering prairie, some literally roasted." The teacher, on the other hand, saved those who stayed at the school by moving the children to an area of plowed prairie.[6]

Home Accidents

Deaths in prairie fires as well as blizzards were dramatic events that remained in the public psyche. But deaths and injuries from fire were far more likely to occur in home accidents. Alice Canfield fell on a hot stove and "burned her back so the skin come off and burned her fingers some but not as bad as her face." As extensive as the injuries seemed to be, she did not die. Neither did a Nebraska boy who set his clothes afire while exploding a bag of black powder. A group of seven- and eight-year-olds escaped the barn they set ablaze while playing "Indian teepee," and Anne Ellis's brother and sister were "two singed, smoky, tear-stained kids" after accidentally igniting a vacant house. The outcome was far different for other families. Two young children died in a barracks fire at Fort Robinson (Nebraska), and "the greatest trouble" in the lives of the McFadin family came when "little sister Mary burned to death in the big fireplace."[7]

Home accidents, which included burns, were common, but death from any sort of accident was less likely than most people believed. In his survey of western Kansas, Elliott West found that only 6 percent of child deaths were the result of accident, and a study of burials in Leavenworth, Kansas, for one year found that only one of 354 child deaths was attributed to an accident (drowning). In Dakota Territory, about one-fifth of the 32 child deaths recorded between June 1869 and June 1870 were attributed to something other than disease or physical problems. There were 2 drownings; 3 children from the same family froze to death; and an eleven-year-old girl was reported as a "suicide" by poison. Of the remaining South Dakota deaths, the cause among older youngsters was assigned to a number of maladies, including pneumonia, diphtheria, scarlet fever, and croup. The younger the child was, the more vague and unidentifiable the cause. Either it was unknown or was attributed to an obvious problem: diarrhea; "tumor on the back," which might have been indicative of some type of birth defect; spasms and "fits," suggesting the possibility of "summer complaint"; and premature birth, including that of triplets, listed as dying soon after delivery. Whatever the cause, it was apparent that children one year of age, or younger, were at the highest risk of becoming a mortality statistic. Making up 55 percent of recorded deaths in the South Dakota data, the youngest were far more likely to succumb to something other than a household accident; in fact there was only one fatality in this age group, that of a one-year-old who fell into a well. Given the incidence of infant mortality, it was little wonder that a frontier doctor observed, "[if a woman] decided she wanted to raise six [children], she would need to bear ten."[8]

Although the numbers for accidental death were low, injuries were part of growing up. There were falls, burns (sometimes from scalding water), and mishaps with farm animals and machinery. Guns came into play too. In just one day a Dallas newspaper reported two accidental shootings involving children. In one a six-year-old wounded both himself and his younger sister when the revolver he was handling discharged. In the other incident a twelve-year-old shot himself in the foot and then, being a "plucky boy," drove himself to town in a buggy to find medical treatment. In these cases, doctors treated the injuries, but parents or neighbors with some doctoring skills were often the nurses, doctors, and surgeons. When "Clarence, a thin frail boy, was thrown from a cow pony, throwing his wrist out of place," his father pulled it back in place and made splints held together with bandages made from a sheet. When a Kansas boy lost part of three fingers while cutting wood, his mother tried to reattach the stumps, and a father amputated a son's leg when it seemed the only thing to save the boy's life from a snakebite.[9]

Considering the prevalence of poisonous snakes on the plains, as well as the frequency of related stories that appear in documentary materials, it is perhaps surprising that relatively few deaths were attributed to snakebites. In his study of Kansas, for example, Elliott West, found only six. West attributed the low number to youngsters knowing the land and its dangers. The same could also be said for bee stings and insect bites, which were more likely to afflict young children who had not yet learned to avoid possible dangers. Mary Leefe vividly recalled her brother's misery when he inadvertently sat on an anthill: "In a moment the ants were swarming over his entire body as he bawled and yelled in anguish." And John Ise described a toddler who "swelled to grotesque proportions" after crawling onto an anthill and receiving multiple bites. Although the child was left in the care of an older sibling while the mother took a few minutes to go to the garden, he managed to escape watchful eyes. Such incidents underscored a common parental fear—children wandering away and being injured or lost on the prairie. Unless accompanied by an adult, Mildred A. Renaud "could not leave the swept area" in front of her South Dakota home, and Oscar Bell, "who was just at the toddling around age," was tied to a bedpost when his mother ventured out onto the North Dakota prairie. She could not take the chance that the boy "would probably follow and get lost."[10]

Child Mortality

A host of dangers demanded caution, but poor nutrition, unsanitary conditions, health problems in newborns, and diseases of all kinds were much more likely to escalate mortality rates. In preterritorial Kansas, the largest number of children, as well as the most births (thirty-six), were in missionary families. Conversely this group also experienced the highest incidence of child deaths (ten children, as opposed to only two recorded among nonmissionary families). The ten ranged in age from one month to eight years, and all the deaths occurred among those born in Kansas rather than any who came to the plains with their parents. Pity the Kerrs and the Johnsons; both couples lost two infants, one after the other, while in Kansas.[11]

Among the other child victims was eight-year-old Charles Lykins, who was one of four, including his mother, to die when an unidentified disease spread through the Wea Baptist Mission. Until the late 1800s there was little understanding of infectious diseases, viral infections, and their correlation to unsanitary conditions and congested living space. Travelers on the Overland Trail, for example, did not equate poor personal hygiene and environmental contamination to cholera outbreaks of the late 1840s and early 1850s. Nor did missionaries realize the health threat posed by crowded mission schools where quarantine policies did not become standard until the close of the 1800s. As a result, early experiences of missionaries in Kansas were repeated elsewhere later in the century. Soon after John J. Read became superintendent of a Choctaw boarding school in Indian Territory in the late 1880s, his daughter died during a pneumonia outbreak among the students, and state institutions for young people, including the Nebraska Girls' Industrial School, experienced repeated outbreaks of pneumonia, scarlet fever, and measles.[12]

Congregated populations were particularly vulnerable to infectious diseases, but a close second were children at military posts. Although officers' families often lived in uncomfortable, poorly constructed housing, the families of enlisted men and post laundresses were far more likely to endure crowded, substandard quarters. At Fort Robinson, for example, an African-American corporal and his wife and child occupied a one-room, windowless shack that the post surgeon declared to be adequately ventilated because an "equal abundance" of light and dirt came through the door. Added to housing problems was the casual dumping of refuse that in turn attracted vermin and contaminated water supplies. Post commanders and surgeons were charged with monitoring and correcting problems, but sanitation at some military installations was a disaster. As a result, diphtheria was a recurring problem at Fort Sill (Oklahoma), and Fort Laramie (Wyoming) saw periodic outbreaks of typhoid fever and diarrhea among children. In addition, several forts lacked an adequate supply and variety of foodstuffs. This created dietary deficiencies and reduced children's ability to resist all sorts of diseases. It was a "miracle," concluded historian Merrill Mattes of Fort Laramie, "[that] post residents were not wiped out by an epidemic." Neither race, education, nor cultural background could overcome man-made environments, crowded conditions, or what the worlds of science and medicine were yet to understand.[13]

As a child, Lettie Little often visited an old cemetery located on the family farm. "Lots of babies were there, even twins," she wrote, "what a price was paid in babies to conquer the frontier." A significant contributor to the loss of the very young was the gastrointestinal condition known by a variety of names—summer complaint, dysentery, cholera infantum. Some believed this to be the leading cause of infant mortality, but most medical officials at the end of the century placed it a close second to a broad category that included death from mishandled deliveries, premature births, birth defects, and stillborns. Summer complaint occurred when weaned toddlers were given cow's or goat's milk and food from the table. Not until the end of the 1800s did science begin to connect gastrointestinal problems to milk or food spoiled by summer's heat and the spread of germs by flies. And it was not until the early twentieth century that studies began to reveal that some immigrant groups, especially those from Germany and Russia, experienced fewer summer complaint deaths because traditional childrearing practices cautioned against feeding solid food before the first birthday. In the population at large, however, the immigrants' approach was not standard, and it was not until the late 1800s that trained physicians began to urge mothers of all backgrounds to extend the period of nursing past what one doctor called "the dread second summer," or to use canned milk, such as the Borden brand, as a substitute. Still, summer complaint persisted. It began with vomiting and diarrhea which then produced dehydration and sometimes fever and convulsions. Some home remedies and doctor prescriptions, such as emetics, compounded the problem. "The result," wrote one progressive doctor, "was a frightful mortality rate. Many a weary night have I spent bathing a child whose convulsions were due to an unsuitable diet, only to lose the battle in the end." The battle continued into the twentieth century, and significant drops in mortality rates were not evident until households routinely screened doors and windows against flies and used some form of reliable refrigeration.[14]

Preventive Medicine

Children of all ages were the victims of contagious diseases such as measles, whooping cough, and scarlet fever. Although homesteaders' children were hardly immune, youngsters in towns and at military posts were more vulnerable. They came into contact with more people on a routine basis, and their surrounding environment was often contaminated by rotting waste and polluted water supplies. As a form of preventive medicine, state governments established departments of public health in the late 1800s, and numerous towns and counties began to designate public health officials (usually a local doctor). Both state and local agencies were charged with enacting and enforcing public health laws and providing health education to a general public that was sometimes complacent and often unwilling to change long-accepted habits and attitudes.

In Western literature, especially the popular Westerns of the twentieth century, "cleaning up" a town meant getting rid of the bawdy houses, gambling halls, and ne'er-do-wells. To those interested in public health and "civilized" living, cleaning up meant something else. Towns along rivers and creeks began to make some effort to keep garbage, excrement, and dead animals out of what was a principal water supply for residents. Many towns began to pass ordinances that required animals to be penned rather than allowed to wander the streets. In some places the laws were meant to contain cattle, horses, or swine, but some, such as Abilene, Kansas, went further and made it a misdemeanor for residents to allow their chickens "to run on other people's property." Confinement laws were long overdue, decided one Dodge City, Kansas, resident who described hogs ambling along sidewalks, standing in doorways, and finding their way with "familiarity" into saloons and dining halls.[15]

Local statutes that attempted to clean up town spaces were only as successful as officials' willingness to enforce the rules and residents' interest in seeing that they did so. Still, public health officials were known to wield considerable authority, especially during times of medical emergency. When smallpox appeared in Dodge City, Kansas, in the early 1890s, the school board, supported by local physicians who made up a loosely organized board of health, ordered all children vaccinated against the disease. Failure to comply barred the child from school, with no exceptions or excuses.[16]

In the nineteenth century, smallpox was one disease that could be prevented through vaccination, but no structured inoculation program existed in the United States, as children in the James Germann family learned firsthand.

> [Father] was also something of a doctor, and we stood around in awe when he came home from Goodland [Kansas] one day with some smallpox serum and prepared to vaccinate us. He sterilized the blade of his pocketknife and used that to scrape the skin so it would absorb the serum. And every one "took" as we can testify today with the scars we still carry.[17]

Despite a known means for preventing smallpox and periodic federal programs to vaccinate Indian groups, localized epidemics occurred in both Euro-American and Native American communities. At an Indian mission in Kansas, a Methodist missionary reported that "while we were sick at the mission, the Indians were suffering equally as much." At times an epidemic was more widespread, leading towns or counties to establish smallpox camps that quarantined the afflicted in one location. Rather than react to outbreaks, health officials tried to encourage inoculation before an epidemic occurred, but public skepticism made it a difficult task. In 1885 the health officer for Marion County, Kansas, reported that "many of the foreign population [German-speaking Mennonites], especially the more ignorant, are greatly adverse to vaccination." Their fears were not unfounded. Some deaths occurred after vaccination. There was the possibility of vaccination scabs becoming badly infected, as happened to two girls inoculated during the Dodge City epidemic. There was also the chance that doctors might make mistakes; in one Kansas county a doctor began a local epidemic by mistakenly using the live virus rather than attenuated vaccine.[18]

As another form of preventive medicine in the late 1800s, towns and counties established quarantine laws that kept sick children out of school and restricted access to patients' homes. When the Beal children came down with diphtheria, "Dr. McIlhenny came out . . . [and] put the red quarantine flag on our gate." Anyone going in could not come out, and those inside remained until the flag, or in some cases the quarantine placard, was removed. Diphtheria, which quarantined the Beals, was not the only disease that brought out the flag, but it was the most deadly, as Elliott West illustrated in his study of Western children. The cause of the disease, an airborne bacterium, was identified in 1883, but this knowledge did not bring a cure or halt outbreaks. Many parents tried the folk remedy of tying a bag of asafetida around a child's neck to prevent the disease; "the smell would discourage a germ of any kind," recalled Rosetta Singley. And more than one physician desperately used any means possible to save patients. In one instance a professionally trained doctor resorted to drenching a boy's mouth and throat with glassfuls of kerosene to break the fibrous membrane that slowly thickened and eventually brought suffocation in such cases. As a result, "the boy [was relieved] and he lived to tell the tale."[19] Unlike the available smallpox vaccine, there was no antitoxin for diphtheria until 1894—the year in which two-year-old Blanche Beal was surely among the first of Western children to be saved by the treatment:

> Dr. McIlhenny said I was so sick nothing could save me unless it might be the new antitoxin he'd read about in the medical journal. No doctor in Sumner County had used it, he said, but if Papa and Mama wanted him to try. . . . So that's what he did. The medicine

worked like a miracle, and the next morning they were all thanking God for the miracle of medicine and for a doctor who wasn't afraid to use it.[20]

By the end of the century, national health-care indicators suggested an overall drop in mortality rates, but the long-held standard that rural children were more likely than urban dwellers to survive their first year remained intact. (The gap between the two narrowed in the early 1900s when health care for the urban poor vastly improved.) Lower rates were attributed to a number of interconnected conditions, including the work of public health officials, urban reformers, public education campaigns, and advances in medical treatment. Preventive measures and a better-educated populace could not ensure a child's survival to adulthood, but the odds were greatly improved.[21]

Home Doctoring

Not every health problem was potentially fatal. Ague was debilitating and made its victims susceptible to other diseases, but it did not kill. Medical theory said that this common complaint among settlers would diminish when land was placed under cultivation, but homesteaders had reason to doubt the promise. DeWitt Clinton Grinell was five years old when he arrived in Kansas in 1859. In 1867, when his neighborhood was crisscrossed with farmsteads and planted fields, he still suffered. Diary entries told the story: "I shook with the Ague. . . . I did not shake but felt pretty bad. . . . I have not shook with the Ague since the 19th." For relief, some sufferers turned to patent medicines or "chill tonics"; Grinell tried Woodward's Ague Cure, with marginal success. More effective in keeping the shakes away was quinine, mixed with whiskey, jelly, or coffee to make it palatable.[22]

Home doctoring used a variety of remedies. Druggists, not all of them medically trained, prepared medicines for customers, and patent medicines were readily available at local stores, through mail order, or at the occasional traveling medicine show. Some patent medicines claimed to treat a specific ailment, but most promised to cure several. Until the first Pure Food and Drug Act was passed in 1906, any patent medicine—adulterated, useless, or lethal—could make any claim and contain any ingredient without consideration for the consumer. As a result, some children were dosed with laudanum (a tincture of opium). The result was sometimes deadly: "I was called to see a baby that was killed by such a nostrum," recalled a frontier doctor who railed against "faker" medicine shows and patent medicines that willfully put profit above safety. In addition to dangerous narcotics, adults dosed themselves and their children with tonics and elixirs that contained substantial levels of alcohol. Diehard prohibitionists and teetotalers would have been appalled at the amount of spirits consumed in their search for a cure.[23]

Despite the availability of patent medicines and those mixed by druggists, Western families relied to a large extent on folk beliefs, medical guidebooks such as *Dr. Chase's Recipes* and *Gunn's Domestic Medicine*, and homemade remedies. Innumerable plants were valued for their medicinal qualities, and items commonly found in the home were used as treatments. Baking powder relieved insect stings and bites. So did mud, which, as in the case of twelve-year-old Sam Dorsey, was also used to draw the poison from snakebite. Kerosene was used to swab inflamed throats, and turpentine was applied to bruises, used to treat snakebites, and mixed with lard and rubbed on sore throats and chests. A variety of teas, from sage and pennyroyal to mullein and sassafras, was employed to settle stomachs, relieve fevers and colds, and treat other childhood ailments. Suffering from the measles, fifteen-year-old Martha Farnsworth complained, "they are soaking me full of tea," and a German girl recalled that "Grandma always made some *Kamille tee* [camomile tea]. . . .

strained it and put the leaves in a rag, then she put it on our [sore] eyes." In late winter and early spring, sassafras tea was administered to counteract the "blood thickening effect of winter," since it was generally believed that the blood had to be "thinned" in order to endure summer's heat. Other "spring tonics" included sorghum and sulfur; sips from a bottle of water filled with rusty nails (an iron additive to the system); and a mixture of sulfur, molasses, and cream of tartar.[24]

Dosages were often administered with the idea "if a little's good, more's better," or on the basis of "best guess." While on his first venture into the fields to bind grain alongside older boys and men, Frank Dean was bitten by a rattlesnake. The boy's grandfather and uncle decided to try a treatment they had recently read about—two tablespoons of spirits of camphor in a cup of milk. Since the men could not recall the exact dosage, Frank drank it all down in one sitting. "Of course with that amount of alcohol I was drunk in a little while and felt no pain. . . . [Then] in spite of the fact that I had already had an overdose . . . I took a second cup of the mixture as per [the found] directions [one teaspoon every half hour]." Given the rather casual attitude toward dosage amounts, it was likely that parents found themselves trying to rescue the victim from the cure.[25]

In the arsenal of home remedies, the poultice held a special place. Used in cases of pneumonia, bronchitis, and croup, poultices were made from a variety of things—boiled onions, flax seed, ground mustard, lard saturated with turpentine, bread and milk, or whatever else was at hand. A teacher at an Indian school in Oklahoma hastily concocted a poultice of boiled potato slices to treat a case of pneumonia, and in about three hours, "[the fever] had gone down entirely and [the girl] went to sleep. . . . After a few hours she was thoroughly relieved." Charles Driscoll, who suffered from croup most winters, was more than a little familiar with "the supreme torture" of mustard poultices and those made with "sizzling fat salt pork in cheesecloth." By spring, when the bouts subsided, his chest "was cooked . . . the skin had blistered and peeled a dozen times." To ward off the croup, Driscoll wore religious medals "hung on a piece of grocery string . . . [and] jingled like a reindeer when I went about the school grounds." Given the teasing he endured for wearing the medals and the pain of fiery poultices, Charles decided that he would have preferred the croup remedy given to a classmate: "George's mother made him drink a cup of his own urine everytime he got an attack of the croup." George was not alone. When all else failed to induce coughing and bring up phlegm, many a frantic mother resorted to urine because it induced vomiting and fits of coughing.[26]

The Shadow of Death

Brushes with life-threatening illnesses or accidents, as well as the deaths of people around them, brought children face-to-face with the specter of mortality. Awareness was reinforced by religious teachings that reminded everyone that death came to all. Intertwined with this message was the promise of an afterlife and the conscious correlation between religious faith and the ability to endure the loss of loved ones. Adults, many guilt-ridden for bringing their children to the plains, turned to religion for comfort. They sought solace in the knowledge that their children had died in a state of grace. When Bertie Canfield, who greeted Kansas with such excitement, died from some unidentified cause two years after homesteading with his family, his mother closed his diary with her own words. "I must record the death of our only son. . . . He was sick nine days, and knew he could not recover, but was calm and resigned having made his peace with God long sence [sic]." Adults clung to a belief in salvation and afterlife to soothe their despair. It was the only thing left, reflected one country doctor who faced grief-stricken parents. "It is life parents want preserved," wrote the doctor. "At such times this transcends the idea of salvation in their minds. . . . Parents do not want their children to go where the minister says they will be better off [heaven]." Still, when death arrived, parents turned to religion and personal faith. As a two-year-old took her last breaths, her Norwegian parents decided that "she looked as if she already beheld Jesus in his glory," and Bertie's mother, visiting her son's grave, thought of an afterlife when the earthly family would be reunited "in the kingdom which is to come."[27]

Historical accounts of early settlements generally list the milestones of a community. Almost inevitably, the first to be born in an area is noted, and often the first funeral is recorded. In more than one instance the first to die was a child. Not long after a group of colonists arrived in Meade County, Kansas, in 1879, little Pearl Atkinson was laid to rest in her "western grave." In another Kansas community the first funeral was that of a boy "who died from the bite of a rattlesnake." For these children the local community came together to observe the culturally accepted forms of mourning, suggesting that even in sparsely populated areas the rituals of death were maintained. Usually members of the extended family and neighbors gathered at the home of the bereaved. They brought food or offered to look after some pressing need such as care of livestock. There were all-night vigils over the deceased and viewing of the body. "The corpse was dressed in her best clothes, and looked very beautiful when we all passed round to take the last look," wrote Percy Ebbutt after attending a wake. Rather than shielding youngsters from death and mourning, adults included them in the rituals. As a teenager, William Lewis was put in charge of funeral arrangements for an infant cousin, and services for young people more often than not included other youngsters. At the "simple, but impressive" funeral of a Kansas teenager, several girls, "former companions" of the deceased, carried the coffin, and at the funeral of a Wichita boy (killed by lightning), "a number of little girls each threw a bouquet of flowers" into the open grave. In many German settlements, girls carried flowers and wreaths in funeral processions, and when the deceased was a child, classmates and child relatives made up a choir. In nineteenth-century America, relatives were expected to show love and devotion by kissing the deceased goodbye. It was an experience that produced traumatic memories for some. Charles Driscoll was only three years old when an older brother died of pneumonia, but over the distance of years he could fully recall the terror of being held over the corpse to kiss his brother's cheek.[28]

In remote areas, funerals were simple. Clergymen were not always present, and coffins were handmade. Nevertheless basic proprieties were observed. When the youngest child of Captain and Mrs. Frederick Benteen died at Fort Rice, Dakota Territory, a soldier made the coffin and a lady at the fort used a piece of her wedding dress to line the plain box. Without a minister, the mourners simply knelt beside the grave and commended "the baby's soul to the Father whence it came." Time and again, settlers recorded the construction of rude coffins, sometimes made by the child's father, and the fabrics contributed as lining. "Mother lined the box with parts from a party dress that she had worn when she was a young woman," recalled one girl. Another remembered her mother and aunt using cotton batting and lace to line the coffin of a neighbor child. For grieving adults, preparing the casket was the last loving act they could provide a lost child.[29]

Where clergy and the trappings of mourning were available, funerals were more elaborate. Immigrant groups held to traditional practices while American-born settlers followed the growing list of appropriate observances dictated by Victorian society. When families could afford it, and sometimes when they could not, caskets and mourning costumes were purchased. Occasionally photographers were hired to capture the last image of a dead child, as well as to photograph family, friends, and siblings gathered around the cas-

The Andrews family gathers at the grave of Willie, who died at the age of nineteen months. *(Solomon D. Butcher Collection, Nebraska State Historical Society)*

ket. The etiquette of bereavement could mystify if not frighten children. A Colorado girl failed to understand the fact of her baby brother's death and her mother's tears. The drama into which she was cast as a central figure in mourning was thrilling, and she felt "quite grand riding in a carriage," a little white coffin at her feet. Charles Driscoll was also impressed by "the majesty of death and its pageantry" represented by a hearse pulled by handsome black horses with black plumes waving over their manes. "What a fine thing it was," he thought, "to get a ride like that, especially since Mother told me that Stephen, having been a good boy, was going straight to heaven."[30]

Religious institutions offered comfort to the bereaved, and popular literature attempted to do the same with memorial poetry and sentimental stories of innocent children who, almost happily, would never have to face the evils and temptations of adulthood. All of this was meant to console, but in one drastic example the promise of heavenly life and the rituals of burial brought terrible tragedy. After attending a child's funeral, six-year-old Willie Sams "manifested a great interest in the burial," wanting to know how the child had gotten into the box and when he would come out. Willie was so taken with the funeral service that he killed his infant brother, buried him in a box, said a prayer, and sang a hymn. The boy then went home, told his mother what he had done, and proudly announced that it was "just like Mr. Arthur's little baby's funeral."[31]

This was an extreme example of child behavior. Nevertheless it conveys the depth of social and religious influence on children. From an early age, children were told that dying was not an end but a prelude to an eternity in heaven. It brought with it the prospect of meeting loved ones again in an afterlife. As an idea that emerged in the early 1800s, this was a decided shift from the harsh Puritan concept of death and the finality expressed through burial. The word "cemetery," which suggested that one simply slept or rested, became more commonly used than "graveyard" and its harsh suggestion of a final end. It is therefore not surprising that a Kansas girl and her siblings "never tired of going up to visit our cemetery friends, old and young." This was no ghoulish childhood fascination but a genuine affection for those represented on the tombstones. Influenced by attitudes of the time, the children regarded the cemetery in the same way as did most nineteenth-century Americans who embraced the Rural Cemetery Movement and its emphasis on peace and beauty in death. The movement, with beginnings in urban areas, was widely accepted. Even in remote areas, residents attempted to imitate the movement's basic emphasis on creating a parklike cemetery environment. Arched and gated entrances represented heaven's "pearly gates." Graveled roadways and paths were lined with plantings. Family outings included cemetery visits, and on Memorial Day entire communities met at local cemeteries. This was the first big celebration in Gutherie, Oklahoma, recalled one resident, despite the fact that the town did not yet have a cemetery or "a single grave to be strewn with flowers." Even without a cemetery, people expected Memorial Day to consist of all-day activities. There were picnic lunches, speeches, music, and the placement of flowers at graves. Strolling among the headstones, visitors recounted the personalities, idiosyncrasies, and virtues of the departed. The cemetery, wrote one historian, was designed "not only to be a decent place for interment, but to serve as a cultural institution." For children, "cemetery friends" were no less real because they were physically absent.[32]

Children seemed to approach the cemetery with a certain detachment, especially when it seemed more like a pleasant park than a place of death. They were, however, aware of death, either through the loss of family members, including brothers and sisters, or the demise of people in the community. Rather than being shielded, youngsters were taught to prepare for the inevitable with religious faith. They were exposed to funeral services and burials, and, while they might revolt against home cures and doctor prescriptions used in times of sickness, they recognized the alternative. When loved ones died, some imitated the popular memorial poetry of the day and wrote their own. Others did not shy away from recording in their diaries and journals deaths or funerals in the neighborhood. DeWitt Clinton Grinell matter-of-factly noted the suicide of "A Negro Living at Henry Barbers," and Henry Norton simply wrote, "Mr. Nicholson's little child died this evening." Youngsters were not impervious to the dangers of accident or disease. Nor were they devoid of emotional compassion and feelings of grief. Rather, they understood death and its meaning in terms of their cultural and religious teachings. Matters of life were also matters of death. In her memorial poem to "the first little brother I ever lost," fourteen-year-old Allie Pettus suggested by her choice of words that she accepted the prospect of other sad losses. It was simply something to expect, as Mary Leefe made clear in describing her first encounter with mortality, "the fact of death registered itself in my baby brain as an incident of life to be expected somewhere, sometime, and somehow."[33]

CHAPTER EIGHT

Common Threads

IN THE SPRING OF 1882, Usher Burdick and his family left Minnesota "for the West."

> Father shipped the stock and implements he had in a box car to Jamestown, Dakota Territory, and I came with my mother on the train. I think the month was May for I remember how the prairie was covered with crocuses. . . . Father filed a claim four miles north-west of Carrington and put up a board shack covered with tar-paper, dug a well and built a small barn.[1]

It was the kind of story told hundreds if not thousands of times, but this was one boy's experience, and his alone. Any personal story is just that—personal and individual. Yet when the single voice becomes a collective chorus with similar circumstances, incidents, and observations repeated time and again, a broader picture emerges of children's experiences on the plains. As participants in Western expansion, they were present early in the century when Euro-Americans attached themselves to only a few forts and Indian missions. They arrived en masse during the process of settlement and town building, and they shared in the emergence of a regional identity that was Western in bent. During their lifetimes, the first children on the plains witnessed the transition from a pre-territorial period to statehood. Alexander Johnson, for example, born in 1832 at Shawnee Methodist Mission, became the youngest member of the first territorial legislature in Kansas, and Elizabeth Simerwell, born in 1835 at the Shawnee Baptist Mission, spent her entire life in Kansas—raising six children, the next generation of Kansans, before her death in 1883.[2] Alexander, Elizabeth, and thousands of others lived during a century of great national development. Youngsters such as Lettie Little, Mary Leefe, William Lewis, and George MacGinitie lived well into the twentieth century, witnessing world wars, the Great Depression, and the most rapid changes in technology yet seen.

For the historical record of nineteenth-century life, children left their diaries and letters. Adults wrote reminiscences and family histories. The result was an extensive and varied vision of Western life. The perceptions of Catherine Wiggins were forever shaded by the death of her father, and, as a result, she called the settlement process "utter futility." George MacGinitie, who was as familiar with the flora and fauna of the prairie as with the built environment, felt sad that "so much of what I experienced as a boy will never again be seen or heard by children," and Jack Heard, growing up on the military frontier of Texas, could not "help but feel sorry for any child not brought up on a post." Josh Wheatcroft, who arrived in Kansas at the age of twelve, waxed poetic: "And sweet are the memories of days gone by/ In the West I've lived and in the West I'll die." Fannie Cole, whose family left Illinois for Kansas in 1855, looked back and still seemed amazed at the experience of settlement: "I was a child, but the journey and the early years of our life in Kansas were so new and strange, so different from anything I could have imagined, that they made an ineradicable impression upon my memory."[3]

Some adults might be accused of sacrificing hard facts for wistful nostalgia or of writing from selective memory, but generally they told both the good and bad, not only to convey personal experience but to explain their place in history. Youngsters writing letters or keeping journals had no motive other than to record what they saw or did. Some exhibited more descriptive flair, and some were more observant or introspective than others. Whether conscious of outside readers or writing for themselves, the writers shared the commonality of being children of the plains. They gathered food and hauled water, walked or rode to school, starred at literary meetings, played baseball or joined a town band, and felt a kinship with the place they called home.

Newly arrived in Nebraska in 1876, a teenage diarist looked around at his community of Swedish migrants and considered the inhospitable weather, lack of fuel, and limited housing. "I have heard no murmur nor words of complaint," he wrote. "Verily the pioneers of Phelps Center are of the stuff of which heroes are made." It was just this sort of attitude that was needed. The diarist and those like him understood that the plains were different, exacting responses of adjustment, perseverance, self-reliance, and cooperation. From the beginning it was also understood that settlement could exact a toll. In 1912 the writer Margaret Hill McCarter made the point in *The Price of the Prairie*, a book of fiction that shared the theme incorporated by other writers who spoke of the price people paid in the loss of loved ones, separated families, and economic setbacks. The "beautiful prairies have been purchased . . . foot by foot," McCarter wrote. It was a price that no one should forget and one that took a greater toll on some than others. A case in point was Maria Peters, a Mennonite in Nebraska. When her father died in 1901 she became acutely aware of how the last twenty-six years in America had passed, and in her mind she returned to the place of her birth: "I am often in Russia with my thoughts, in a time a long time ago when we still attended school." Separation from "home" and tensions between traditional immigrant parents and assimilated Americanized children was, wrote the novelist O. E. Rölvaag, the "tragedy of emigration."[4]

Immigrants paid the price, but the degree of cultural disintegration, as well as incidents of bigotry and racism, varied considerably.

The West constituted a pluralistic society riddled with ironies. Celebrated on one hand as a place where character transcended class, social standing, or material wealth, it expected, as did all of American society, assimilation and acculturation. As a result, immigrant groups and African Americans made accommodations and joined with the dominant society while also trying to preserve distinctive features of language and tradition. Thus people identified themselves in terms of race and ethnicity as well as part of the larger frontier experience that ensured Western development.

Death, droughts, blizzards, boom-bust economics, and failed towns were part of plains living. "[Children] saw the gambles of life and the size of the stakes," wrote Mari Sandoz. "They shared in the privation and the hard work." A litany of things could and did adversely affect children. Childhood narratives recorded them, and adult reminiscences recalled them. Taken alone, the accounts project a dark picture, but that was not the breadth of perceptions or experience. Interwoven were good times, silly antics, love of the land, and outright optimism. In fact, hard times were often related within the context of overcoming obstacles. Some might call this Western bravado, but there was a decided mind-set that took pride in living in a "hard place" and meeting a challenge. There was the optimistic refrain of "wait 'till next year." "Usually the impression is conveyed that the pioneers were an unhappy lot of people," said an Oklahoma women, "[but] those were happy days. . . . They were in good spirits, they had a hope for the future." Added a woman who grew up in western Kansas, "We always planned on next year being a good year and never quite gave up."[5]

Children born in the plains environment and those who arrived from other parts of the United States or from Europe related to the region in terms of birthplace or new home, and their childhoods were shaped in part by specific events of time and place in Western development. Migrants adopted the plains as their home. For those born there, the West was what a twentieth-century Westerner called the "navel of the world." Nevertheless they shared a common feeling that they were part of a historic moment in a place that made no promises for easy living. The Western society in which these children grew up segregated people into two broad categories: those who "stuck" and those who turned and ran in the face of adversity. Social commentators argued that hardships weeded out the people who did not belong. In effect, Social Darwinism was at work. Those who remained were told, and believed, that they were a special breed. Not only did they stick as individuals, but hardships bound them together. George Thompson, a child in Nebraska, firmly held to this view when he wrote that adversity produced a mutual sympathy among settlers "of any race or creed."[6]

Children growing up on the plains were sometimes portrayed as wild, like the land. To an outside observer, children were too undisciplined and independent. Girls, in particular, were missing the socializing messages of gender-specific behavior. The view was badly distorted. Blurred gender roles at work, and sometimes play, did not overturn male and female spheres, though loosened roles in childhood served both boys and girls with a strong sense of self-confidence when they entered adulthood. Social order could indeed be found on the plains, transplanted by adults and reinforced by the social, educational, and religious institutions established in rural communities and towns. Schools, libraries, and churches were organized with children in mind, and youngsters were at the center of holiday celebrations, school programs, and literary meetings. Hours spent at essential chores were offset by play. Much of the latter was of children's own making, but parents, especially mothers, seriously directed playtime activities as part of their childrearing responsibilities. Cultural values, whether immigrant or American Victorian, contained strongly stated expectations for family life, parental and community responsibilities to children, and the transmittal of beliefs to the next generation. Considerable time and energy were directed toward children, their education, religious instruction, and social interactions.

By the late 1800s children may not have collected cow chips for fuel or felt anxiety over Indian-white relations, but they were not far removed from those who had. Through family stories, including those of their parents and those told by older members of the community, late-nineteenth-century children heard personal and local histories of grasshopper plagues, railroad building, military life, and cattle trails. Many continued to know frontier conditions firsthand. Those who did not shared others' experiences, if only vicariously. When youngsters added these to their personal catalogues of perceptions and facts of daily existence, the continuity of frontier life, even if frontier conditions no longer existed, became part of their identities. They were not, and had not been, passive spectators to the Western experience.

Notes

Introduction

1. Louise Barry, comp., *The Beginning of the West: Annals of the Kansas Gateway to the American West, 1540–1854* (Topeka: Kansas State Historical Society, 1972), 155; "Kansas or Hodgeman County as Seen by a Little Girl (Mrs. S. S. Button)," *Jetmore* [Kans.] *Republican*, April 25, 1930, 1.

2. Merrill J. Mattes, *The Great Platte River Road: The Covered Wagon Mainline Via Fort Kearny to Fort Laramie* (Lincoln: Nebraska State Historical Society, 1969; reprint, Lincoln: University of Nebraska Press, 1987); Emmy E. Werner, *Pioneer Children on the Journey West* (Boulder, Colo.: Westview Press, 1995); Susan Arrington Madsen, *I Walked to Zion: True Stories of Young Pioneers on the Mormon Trail* (Salt Lake City: Deseret Book Co., 1994); Elizabeth Hampsten, *Settlers' Children: Growing Up on the Great Plains* (Norman: University of Oklahoma Press, 1991); Cathy Luchetti, *Children of the West: Family Life on the Frontier* (New York: Norton, 2001); Patricia Y. Stallard, *Glittering Misery: Dependents of the Indian Fighting Army* (Fort Collins, Colo.: Old Army Press, 1978; reprint, Norman: University of Oklahoma Press, 1992); Elliott West, *Growing Up with the Country: Childhood on the Far-Western Frontier* (Albuquerque: University of New Mexico Press, 1989).

3. Frederick C. Luebke, "Ethnic Group Settlement on the Great Plains," *Western Historical Quarterly* 8 (October 1977), 405.

4. Mollie Dorsey Sanford, *Mollie: The Journal of Mollie Dorsey Sanford in Nebraska and Colorado Territories, 1857–1866* (Lincoln: University of Nebraska Press, 1976), 2.

5. Ian Frazier, *Great Plains* (New York: Viking Penguin, 1990), 7; Jim Hoy and Tom Isern, *Plain Folks, II: The Romance of the Landscape* (Norman: University

of Oklahoma Press, 1990), viii; Paula M. Nelson, "The First Hundred Years Are the Hardest: The Ironies of Great Plains Life, 1870–1991," 2, pamphlet, College of Arts and Sciences Banquet Address, University of Wisconsin–Platteville, October 25, 1991.

6. Enid Bern, "The Enchanted Years on the Prairies," _North Dakota History_ 40 (Fall 1973), 5; Josephine Boltz, "I Remember," 1, typescript, Lane County Historical Society, Dighton, Kans.

Chapter 1. Perceptions and Expectations

1. Rolf Johnson, _Happy as a Big Sunflower: Adventures in the West_, ed. Richard E. Jensen (Lincoln: University of Nebraska Press, 2000), 13, 14.
2. Barry, _Beginning of the West_, 145, 151, 155.
3. _Illinois Bounty Land Register_, Quincy, Ill., April 17, 1835, 1.
4. Stallard, _Glittering Misery_, 57; Barry, _Beginning of the West_, 327–328, 511.
5. Barry, _Beginning of the West_, 168, 318, 424; Daniel D. Holt and Marilyn Irvin Holt, " 'The Pleasures of Female Society' at Cantonment Leavenworth," _Kansas History_ 8 (Spring 1985), 28.
6. Daniel Beekman, _The Mechanical Baby: A Popular History of the Theory and Practice of Child Raising_ (Westport, Conn.: Laurence Hill & Co., 1977), 55; Lydia Child, _The Mother's Book_ (Boston: Carter and Hendee, 1831; reprint, New York: Arno Press and the New York Times, 1972), 3, 60, 93. Among magazine articles, see "The Young Mother," _Godey's Magazine and Lady's Book_ 37 (November 1848), 253–254; "Little Children," _Godey's Magazine and Lady's Book_ 48 (March 1854), 207; "Home Training of Children," _Monthly Religious Magazine_ 10 (January 1853), 24; and William C. Brown, "Tendency of Punishments," _The Mother's Assistant and Young Lady's Friend_ 1 (April 1841), 84.
7. Elizabeth B. Custer, _"Boots and Saddles" or Life in Dakota with General Custer_ (New York: Harper & Brothers, 1885; reprint, New York: Harper & Brothers, 1901), 99; Ray H. Mattison, ed., "An Army Wife on the Upper Missouri: The Diary of Sarah E. Canfield, 1866–1868," _North Dakota History_ 20 (October 1953), 213; Philip St. George Cooke, _Scenes and Adventures in the Army; or, Romance of Military Life_ (Philadelphia: Lindsay and Blakiston, 1857), 40, 93.
8. William H. Collins, _The Collins Family_ (Quincy, Ill.: Volk, Jones and McMein, 1897), 162; Alice Mathews Shields, "Army Life on the Wyoming Frontier," _Annals of Wyoming_ 13 (October 1941), 332–333, 334; Mary Leefe Laurence, _Daughter of the Regiment: Memoirs of a Childhood in the Frontier_

Army, 1878–1898, ed. Thomas T. Smith (Lincoln: University of Nebraska Press, 1996), 85.

9. Horace Greeley, *An Overland Journey from New York to San Francisco in the Summer of 1859*, ed. Charles T. Duncan (New York: Alfred A. Knopf, 1964), 63; Anne Ellis, *The Life of an Ordinary Woman* (Boston: Houghton Mifflin 1929; reprint, Boston: Houghton Mifflin, 1990), 13; Marian Russell, *Land of Enchantment: Memoirs of Marian Russell Along the Santa Fe Trail as Dictated to Mrs. Hal Russell*, ed. Garnet M. Brayer (Evanston, Ill.: Branding Iron Press, 1954; reprint, Albuquerque: University of New Mexico Press, 1981), xii, 18, 90, 93.

10. Barry, *Beginning of the West*, 180; "The Cherokee Nation's First White Orphan Home—Compiled from Old Documents Left by the Late Rev. W. A. Duncan," 457–458, vol. 83, Indian-Pioneer History Project, WPA Collection, Oklahoma Historical Society, Oklahoma City (hereinafter cited as IP, Oklahoma); Custer, *"Boots and Saddles,"* 125–126; Catharine Hertzog to Michael Baker, August 1829 and December 21, 1831, Morris Collection, Illinois State Historical Library, Springfield.

11. "An Interview with Mrs. Thomas Ballard," 224, vol. 14, IP, Oklahoma; Clara Ewell, *Ten Years of My Life* (author, 1973), 7.

12. Mattes, *Great Platte River Road*, 239; Robert W. Richmond, *Kansas, A Land of Contrasts* (St. Charles, Mo.: Forum Press, 1974), 21; Mody C. Boatright, *Folk Laughter on the American Frontier* (New York: Macmillan, 1949; reprint, New York: Collier, 1961), 164.

13. J. H. Beadle, *The Undeveloped West; or, Five Years in the Territories . . .* (Philadelphia: National Publishing Co., 1873), 81.

14. David Emmons, *Garden in the Grasslands: Boomer Literature of the Central Great Plains* (Lincoln: University of Nebraska Press, 1971), chap. 6; C. D. Wilber, *The Great Valleys and Prairies of Nebraska and the Northwest* (Omaha: Daily Republican, 1881), 143; *Commonwealth*, Topeka, Kans., November 25, 1880, 3; Hugh R. Hilton, "Kansas and Its Supply of Moisture," *Prairie Farmer*, Chicago, April 19 and 26, May 3, 1879.

15. Ellen May Stanley, *Cowboy Josh: Adventures of a Real Cowboy* (Newton, Kans.: Mennonite Press, 1996), 17; Hamlin Garland, *A Son of the Middle Border* (New York: Macmillan, Modern Readers' Series ed., 1923), 220.

16. James F. Walker, "Old Fort Berthold as I Knew It," *North Dakota History* 20 (January 1953), 26; "The Adams-Kimbrel Families," in *Dodge City and Ford County, Kansas, Pioneer Histories and Stories, 1870–1920* (Dodge City: Ford County Historical Society, 1996), 87; John Talcott Norton Diary, March 25

and April 30, 1878, Norton Family Diaries, 1876–1895, Manuscripts, Kansas State Historical Society, Topeka (hereinafter cited as MS, KSHS); Sanford, *Journal of Mollie Dorsey Sanford*, 3; David G. Siceloff, *Boy Settler in the Cherokee Strip* (Caldwell, Idaho: Caxton Printers, 1964), 11.

17. "Grace Russell Shouse," *Dighton* [Kans.] *Herald*, January 23, 1957, 3; James Shortridge, *The Middle West: Its Meaning in American Culture* (Lawrence: University Press of Kansas, 1989), 28–29; Richard H. Abbott, "The Agricultural Press Views the Yeoman: 1819–1859," *Agricultural History* 42 (January 1968), 35–48; *Smith County Kansas Pioneer*, Smith Center, Kans., March 21, 1879; Siceloff, *Boy Settler*, 46.

18. J. A. Riis, "Christmas Reminder of the Noblest Work in the World," *Forum* 16 (January 1894), 624; Ella Guernsey, "Letters from the People," *New Era* 1 (April 1885), 121–122.

19. Stanley, *Cowboy Josh*, 25, 29; "Clark County Historical Society Notes," *Clark County Clipper*, Ashland, Kans., December 14, 1939, 2; Harry Colwell, *Growing Up in Old Kansas* (Houston, Tex.: D. Armstrong Co., 1985), 5.

20. Alma Carlson Roosa, "Homesteading in the 1880's: The Anderson-Carlson Families of Cherry County," ed. Henry W. and Jean Tyree Hamilton, *Nebraska History* 58 (Fall 1977), 386; Fannie E. Cole, "Pioneer Life in Kansas," *Kansas Historical Collections* 12 (1911–1912), 355; Shields, "Army Life on the Wyoming Frontier," 332; Walker, "Old Fort Berthold," 34.

21. Craig Miner, *West of Wichita: Settling the High Plains of Kansas, 1865–1890* (Lawrence: University Press of Kansas, 1986), 18–22; James T. King, "Forgotten Pageant—The Indian Wars in Western Nebraska," *Nebraska History* 46 (September 1965), 183–185; John D. Unruh, Jr., *The Plains Across: The Overland Emigrants and the Trans-Mississippi West, 1840–60* (Urbana: University of Illinois Press, Illini Books, 1982), 149; Daniel D. Holt, "Lieutenant Frank D. Baldwin and the Indian Territory Expedition of 1874," *Trail Guide* 10 (September 1965), 12–16.

22. Sherry L. Smith, *The View from Officer's Row: Army Perceptions of Western Indians* (Tucson: University of Arizona Press, 1990), 76; Shields, "Army Life on the Wyoming Frontier," 332, 334; Dorothy Dueker, "Pioneering on Snake Creek," in *Pioneer Tales of the North Platte Valley and Nebraska Panhandle*, comp. A. B. Wood (Gering, Nebr.: Courier Press, 1938), 84–86; Laurence, *Daughter of the Regiment*, 7–9, 12, 19, 21.

23. Laurence, *Daughter of the Regiment*, 18–19, 150; Walker, "Old Fort Berthold," 34–35.

24. Don Russell, ed., "Julia Cody Goodman's Memoir of Buffalo Bill," *Kansas Historical Quarterly* 28 (Winter 1962), 453; "Covered Wagon Diary," in *"A Funnie Place, No Fences": Teenagers' Views of Kansas, 1867–1900*, eds. C. Robert Haywood and Sandra Jarvis (Lawrence: Division of Continuing Education, University of Kansas, 1992), 20, 21; Norman E. Saul, "The Migration of the Russian-Germans to Kansas," *Kansas Historical Quarterly* 40 (Spring 1974), 56, 58; "Immigrant Contingent," *Nebraska Daily State Journal*, Lincoln, July 29, 1874, 2; "The Mennonites," *Commonwealth*, Topeka, Kans., September 10, 1874, 2; Royden Loewen, *Hidden Worlds: Revisiting the Mennonite Migrants of the 1870s* (North Newton, Kans.: Bethel College, 2001), 54–57. For stories on Volga Germans, see Isadore Appelhanz, comp., "Topeka Newspapers: Volga-German Arrivals in 1875," *Journal of the American Historical Society of Germans from Russia* 21 (Summer 1998), 16–29.

25. George E. MacGinitie, *The Not So Gay Nineties: An Account of Childhood in Lynch, Nebraska, As It Was Eighty Years Ago* (author, 1972), 185; Charles B. Driscoll, *Kansas Irish* (New York: Macmillan, 1943), 314; Lettie Little Pabst, *Kansas Heritage* (New York: Vantage Press, 1956), 146.

26. Ovella Dunn to Annie Moore, December 3, 1869, Harriet Ovella Dunn Letters, MS, KSHS; Willie Newbury Lewis, *Tapadero: The Making of a Cowboy* (Austin: University of Texas Press, 1972), 6–7.

27. Bob Kennon, *From the Pecos to the Powder: A Cowboy's Autobiography* (Norman: University of Oklahoma Press, 1965), 12; Ovella Dunn to Annie Moore, November 3, December 3, 1869, MS, KSHS; "A Funnie Place, No Fences," in *"A Funnie Place, No Fences,"* 6–7.

28. Sanford, *Journal of Mollie Dorsey Sanford*, 13, 15, 32.

29. George B. Thompson, "Pioneering on the Nebraska Prairies," 1, typescript, Manuscripts, Nebraska State Historical Society, Lincoln (hereinafter cited as MS, NSHS); "Coming to Kansas," in *"Funnie Place, No Fences,"* 1–2.

30. Russell, *Land of Enchantment*, 22; Stanley, *Cowboy Josh*, 24.

31. MacGinitie, *Not So Gay Nineties*, 8.

32. Lewis, *Tapadero*, 3, 6; Mattes, *Great Platte River Road*, 220; Johnson, *Happy as a Big Sunflower*, 11.

33. Joanna L. Stratton, *Pioneer Women: Voices from the Kansas Frontier* (New York: Simon and Schuster, 1981), 56; "Memories of Agnes Krom Quick," in *Dodge City and Ford County, Kansas*, 75–76; *Topeka Capital*, August 29, 1937; "Mrs. S. S. Button," *Jetmore* [Kans]. *Republican*, April 25, 1930, 1; Siceloff, *Boy Settler*, 26.

34. Martin Ridge, ed., *Frederick Jackson Turner: Wisconsin's Historian of the Frontier* (Madison: State Historical Society of Wisconsin, 1986), 26, 30; MacGinitie, *Not So Gay Nineties*, 226–227; Ewell, *Ten Years of My Life*, 26.

Chapter 2. Travel and Settlement

1. Robber's Roost Historical Society and Sylvie Hogg Marchant, comps., *Pioneering on the Cheyenne River* (Lusk, Wyo.: Lusk Herald, 1947), 81–82.
2. Percy G. Ebbutt, *Emigrant Life in Kansas* (London: Swan Sonnenschein and Co., 1886), 1–4.
3. Johnson, *Happy as a Big Sunflower*, xix; C. Robert Haywood, "The Hodgeman County Colony," *Kansas History* 12 (Winter 1989–1990): 210-21; "Our Colony," *Pearlette* [Kans.] *Call*, April 15, 1879, 1.
4. Gary D. Olson, "The Historical Background of Land Settlement in Eastern South Dakota," in *Big Sioux Pioneers: Essays About the Settlement of the Dakota Prairie Frontier*, ed. Arthur R. Huseboe (Sioux Falls, S.D.: Norland Heritage Foundation, 1980), 19; Richmond, *Kansas, A Land of Contrasts*, 160; Lewis, *Tapadero*, 3, 117; Cole, "Pioneer Life in Kansas," 353; Mari Sandoz, *Love Song to the Plains* (New York: Harper & Brothers, 1961), 146, 150; John W. Reps, *The Forgotten Frontier: Urban Planning in the American West Before 1890* (Columbia: University of Missouri Press, 1981), 66–76; James R. Shortridge, "People of the New Frontier: Kansas Population Origins, 1865," *Kansas History* 14 (Autumn 1991), 183; Greeley, *An Overland Journey*, 55.
5. Daniel D. Wilder, "Where Kansans Were Born," *Kansas State Historical Society Collections* 9 (1905–1906), 506–508; Eleanor L. Turk, "Selling the Heartland: Agents, Agencies, Press and Policies in Promoting German Emigration to Kansas in the Nineteenth Century," *Kansas History* 12 (Autumn 1989), 156–158; Ronald A. Wells, "Migration and the Image of Nebraska in England," *Nebraska History* 54 (Fall 1973), 475–491; Lawrence H. Konecny and Clinton Machann, "German and Czech Immigration to Texas: The Bremen to Galveston Route, 1880–1886," *Nebraska History* 74 (Fall–Winter 1993), 136–141; J. Neale Carman, trans., "German Settlements Along the Atchison, Topeka and Santa Fe Railway: A Translation from the German," *Kansas Historical Quarterly* 28 (Autumn 1962), 312–316.
6. Luebke, "Ethnic Group Settlement," 410; Turk, "Selling the Heartland," 150, 156–158; Tarrel R. Miller, *The Dakotans* (Stickney, S.D.: Argus Printers, 1964),

102; J. Sanford Rikoon, "Jewish Farm Settlements in America's Heartland," in *Rachel Calof's Story: Jewish Homesteader on the Northern Plains*, ed. J. Sanford Rikoon (Bloomington: Indiana University Press, 1995), 117; Harold E. Briggs, "The Great Dakota Boom, 1879 to 1886," *North Dakota Historical Quarterly* 4 (January 1930), 88–89.

7. Rosa Kleberg, "Some of My Early Experiences in Texas," trans. Rudolph Kleberg Jr., *Quarterly of the Texas State Historical Association* 1 (April 1898), 299, 305–306; Hampsten, *Settlers' Children*, 70–71; Elwyn B. Robinson, *History of North Dakota* (Lincoln: University of Nebraska Press, 1966), 170.

8. Miller, *The Dakotas*, 102; "Immigrant Contingent," *Nebraska Daily State Journal*, Lincoln, July 29, 1874, 2; Richmond, *Kansas, A Land of Contrasts*, 149, 163.

9. Haywood and Jarvis, *"A Funnie Place, No Fences,"* 2; *Chronicle*, Abilene, Kans., November 30, 1871, 2; Stanley, *Cowboy Josh*, 29–30; Kenneth Wiggins Porter, ed., " 'Holding Down' a Northwest Kansas Claim, 1885–1888," *Kansas Historical Quarterly* 22 (Autumn 1956), 220–221.

10. Sanford, *Journal of Mollie Dorsey Sanford*, 4–11; "A Funnie Place, No Fences," in *"A Funnie Place, No Fences,"* 5–6; Lewis, *Tapadero*, 3, 6; Laurence, *Daughter of the Regiment*, 66.

11. Stratton, *Pioneer Women*, 59–60; Robber's Roost Historical Society, *Pioneering on the Cheyenne River*, 87; Lem Pogue, "The Last Buffalo," *Jetmore* [Kans.] *Republican*, April 25, 1930, 1; "Clark County Historical Society Notes," *Clark County Clipper*, Ashland, Kans., December 14, 1939, 2; "Mrs. S. S. Button," *Jetmore* [Kans.] *Republican*, April 25, 1930, 1; "The Adams-Kimbrel Families," in *Dodge City Pioneer Stories*, 87–88. Census records support family separation; the 1880 U.S. Census, Lane County, Kans., for example, lists three "farmers" with "families back East."

12. Gary D. Olson, "The Historical Background of Land Settlement in Eastern South Dakota," in *Big Sioux Pioneers*, 24, 27; *U.S. Census, 1890, Population, pt. 3* (Washington, D.C.: Government Printing Office), 468–469; Richmond, *Kansas, A Land of Contrasts*, 149, 151; Sara L. Bernson and Robert J. Eggers, "Black People in South Dakota History," *South Dakota History* 7 (Summer 1977), 249, 251; Jon Gjerde, *The Minds of the West: Ethnocultural Evolution in the Rural Middle West, 1830–1917* (Chapel Hill: University of North Carolina Press, 1997), 22, 63, 163; Sheridan County, Kans., U.S. Census, 1880.

13. E. M. Angell, "A. V. Angell Family: Pioneer Days in Western Kansas, Meade County," 8, 9, and Rosetta Singley, "A Pioneer Family—Mr. and Mrs. R. R.

Singley," 214, in *Pioneer Stories of Meade County*, comp. Council of Women's Clubs (Meade, Kans.: Council of Women's Clubs, 1965).

14. Waldemar C. Westergaard, "History of the Danish Settlement in Hill Township, Cass County, North Dakota," *North Dakota Historical Society Collections* 1 (1906), 159; Ebbutt, *Emigrant Life in Kansas*, 17–18.

15. W. E. Cox, "Reflections of Early Days in Saline County," 7–8, typescript, MS, NSHS.

16. Richmond, *Kansas, A Land of Contrasts*, 135; Kansas Preservation Department, *Kansas Preservation Plan: Study Unit on the Period of Exploration and Settlement (1820s–1880s)* (Topeka: Kansas State Historical Society, 1987), 62, 65; Carolyn Sands, "Frontier Architecture of the Big Sioux Valley: 1865–1885," in *Big Sioux Pioneers*, 33–34.

17. Ewell, *Ten Years of My Life*, 27; Sands, "Frontier Architecture," in *Big Sioux Pioneers*, 31, 33; U.S. Department of the Interior, National Park Service, *Promised Land on the Solomon: Black Settlement at Nicodemus, Kansas* (Washington, D.C.: Government Printing Office, 1985), 8, 27, fn46; Mrs. M. L. Sterrett, "Negro Colony Among Early Settlers of Hodgeman County," *Jetmore* [Kans.] *Republican*, April 25, 1930, 2.

18. Rikoon, *Rachel Calof's Story*, 24–25; Robert Leonard Ligon, *Just Dad: A Pioneer History of the Southwest* (Schenectady, N.Y.: Character Research Press, 1976), 17; George C. Anderson, "Touring Kansas and Colorado in 1871: The Journal of George C. Anderson," *Kansas Historical Quarterly* 22 (Autumn 1956), 193, 197, 199, 216; A. G. Burr, "Some Highlights of Bottineau County History," *North Dakota History* 16 (October 1949), 219.

19. Usher L. Burdick, "Recollections and Reminiscences of Graham's Island," *North Dakota History* 16 (January 1949), 9; Charley O'Kieffe, *Western Story: The Recollections of Charley O'Kieffe, 1884–1898* (Lincoln: University of Nebraska Press, 1960), 7; Stanley, *Cowboy Josh*, 13–14.

20. Adelia Clifton, "A Pioneer Family in Old Greer County," *Chronicles of Oklahoma* 39 (Summer 1961), 156; Miller, *The Dakotans*, 104–106; Sands, "Frontier Architecture," in *Big Sioux Pioneers*, 31; U. S. Department of the Interior, *Promised Land on the Solomon*, 37.

21. Stratton, *Pioneer Women*, 55.

22. Singley, "A Pioneer Family," in *Pioneer Stories of Meade County*, 214.

23. Clifton, "A Pioneer Family in Old Greer County," 157; John C. Jones and Winoma C. Jones, *Prairie Pioneers of Western Kansas and Eastern Colorado* (Boulder, Colo.: Johnson Publishing Co., 1956), 54; Sallie Reynolds

Matthews, *Interwoven: A Pioneer Chronicle* (College Station: Texas A & M University Press, 1982), 29; Ellis, *Life of an Ordinary Woman*, 42; Samuel J. Crumbine, *Frontier Doctor: The Autobiography of a Pioneer on the Frontier of Public Health* (Philadelphia: Dorrance & Co., 1948), 56–57.

24. O'Kieffe, *Western Story*, 62; Sara J. Keckeisen, "Cottonwood Ranch: John Fenton Pratt and the English Ranching Experience in Sheridan County, Kansas," *Kansas History* 14 (Spring 1991), 41–42; Laurence, *Daughter of the Regiment*, 28; Frank N. Schubert, *Buffalo Soldiers, Braves and the Brass: The Story of Fort Robinson, Nebraska* (Shippensburg, Pa.: White Mane Publishing Co., 1993), 58–61; Miller J. Stewart, "Army Laundresses: Ladies of the 'Soap Suds Row,'" *Nebraska History* 61 (Winter 1980), 422–423.

25. Alvar W. Carlson, "German-Russian Houses in Western North Dakota," *Pioneer America* 13 (September 1981), 58; Saul, "Migration of the Russian-Germans to Kansas," 57; David V. Wiebe, *They Seek a Country: A Survey of Mennonite Migrations with Special Reference to Kansas and Gnadenau* (Hillsboro, Kans.: Mennonite Brethren Publishing House, 1959), 145–148; "Homes! Homes!" *Attwood* [Kans.] *Pioneer*, October 23, 1879, 1 (the town spelling is now Atwood).

26. Duane A. Smith, *Rocky Mountain West: Colorado, Wyoming, & Montana, 1859–1915* (Albuquerque: University of New Mexico Press, 1992), vii; Briggs, "Great Dakota Boom," 90; Shortride, "People of the New Frontier," 183; Cox, "Reflections of the Early Days in Saline County," 23, MS, NSHS.

27. Richmond, *Kansas, A Land of Contrasts*, 120; *Union*, Junction City, Kans., July 8, 1871.

28. *Union*, Junction City, Kans., July 8, 1871; "Gala Hall," *Star-Sentinel*, Hays City, Kans., July 9, 1885, 1.

29. C. Robert Haywood, *Victorian West: Class and Culture in Kansas Cattle Towns* (Lawrence: University Press of Kansas, 1991), 87; *Kearney* [Nebr.] *Daily Hub*, May 2, 1891, 1; Richard Thornton, "Boom Town, Kearney," *Nebraska History* 34 (April–June 1943), 110.

30. Reuben Hill, "The American Family Today," 6, typescript, box 120, Workgroups 39–42 file, White House Conferences on Children and Youth: Records, 1930–1970, Dwight D. Eisenhower Presidential Library, Abilene, Kans. (hereinafter cited as White House Conferences, DDE); Kellee Green, "The Fourteenth Numbering of the People: The 1920 Federal Census," *Prologue: Quarterly of the National Archives* 23 (Summer 1991), 131–132; Lowe, "Growing Up in Kansas," 49.

31. L. O. McHenry, "Historical Reminiscence by Native Son of Valley," in *Pioneer Tales of the North Platte Valley and Nebraska Panhandle*, 55; MacGinitie, *Not So Gay Nineties*, 13.

32. Pabst, *Kansas Heritage*, 146–147; Della Knowles Diary, June 21, 1892, Kansas Collection, Spencer Library, University of Kansas, Lawrence, Kans. (hereinafter cited as Kansas Collection); Ellis, *Life of an Ordinary Woman*, 88; Driscoll, *Kansas Irish*, 235.

33. Willard B. Gatewood, Jr., "Kate D. Chapman Reports on 'The Yankton Colored People,' 1889," *South Dakota History* 7 (Winter 1976), 28–35; Bernson and Eggers, "Black People in South Dakota History," 250.

34. Kenneth Wiggins Porter, ed., "Catherine Emma Wiggins, Pupil and Teacher in Northwest Kansas, 1888–1895," *Kansas History* 1 (Spring 1978), 18; Marion Lyon Faegre, "Habits of Independence," 4–5, White House Conference Leaflets, Series on Habits V., 1930, box 1, folder 2, White House Conferences, DDE.

Chapter 3. Family and Community

1. Laurence, *Daughter of the Regiment*, 29–30; Schubert, *Buffalo Soldiers, Braves, and the Brass*, 62.

2. Betty G. Farrell, *Family: The Making of an Idea, an Institution, and a Controversy in American Culture* (Boulder, Colo.: Westview Press, 1999), 6–7; Carl N. Degler, *At Odds: Woman and Family in America from the Revolution to the Present* (New York: Oxford University Press, 1980), chap. 1; Tamara Hareven, "The History of the Family and the Complexity of Social Change," *American Historical Review* 96 (February 1991), 96–97, 105, 108.

3. Pabst, *Kansas Heritage*, 30; Walter Johnson, *William Allen White's America* (New York: Henry Holt, 1947), 24.

4. Robert C. Ostergren, "The Immigrant Church as a Symbol of Community and Place in the Upper Midwest," *Great Plains Quarterly* 1 (Fall 1981), 228; "Kingman County," *Second Biennial Report of the State Board of Agriculture to the Legislature of the State of Kansas, 1879–80* (Topeka: Geo. W. Martin, Kansas Publishing House, 1881), 359, 522; "Mrs. T. A. Arnold Interview," 465, vol. 12, IP, Oklahoma; Glenda Riley, ed., "Kansas Frontierswomen Viewed Through Their Writings: The Journal of Carrie Robbins," *Kansas History* 9 (Autumn 1986), 141; West, *Growing Up with the Country*, 169–170; Frank W. Dean, "Pi-

oneering in Nebraska, 1872–1879: A Reminiscence," *Nebraska History* 36 (June 1955), 105.

5. MacGinitie, *Not So Gay Nineties*, 127; Driscoll, *Kansas Irish*, 116; Della Knowles Diary, August 7, 1892, Kansas Collection; Ebbutt, *Emigrant Life in Kansas*, 123–124; John Ise, *Sod and Stubble: The Story of a Kansas Homestead* (New York: Wilson Erickson, 1936; reprint, Lincoln: University of Nebraska Press, 1970), 245–246; Pabst, *Kansas Heritage*, 28.

6. Nupur Chaudhuri, "'We All Seem Like Brothers and Sisters': The African-American Community in Manhattan, Kansas, 1865–1940," *Kansas History* 14 (Winter 1991–1992), 277; Russell, *Land of Enchantment*, 21; Laurence, *Daughter of the Regiment*, 30, 100; Ellen May Stanley, "Prairie Home Companions," *Kansas Heritage* 9 (Summer 2001), 15.

7. "Attempted Kidnapping," *Albany* [Tex.] *Echo*, September 5, 1883, 5; Lewis, *Tapadero*, 55–56; John Talcott Norton Diary, October 28, 1877, and January 12, 1878, MS, KSHS; Stallard, *Glittering Misery*, 80; Ellis, *Life of an Ordinary Woman*, 40–41.

8. Ise, *Sod and Stubble*, 240; MacGinitie, *Not So Gay Nineties*, 179; Pabst, *Kansas Heritage*, 25; Driscoll, *Kansas Irish*, 79–82.

9. Cox "Reflections of Early Days in Saline County," 18, MS, NSHS; West, *Growing Up with the Country*, 168.

10. Richmond, *Kansas, A Land of Contrasts*, 149; *Buckner Independent*, Jetmore, Kans., August 19, 1880; "Memories of Agnes Krom Quick," in *Dodge City and Ford County, Kansas*, 77.

11. Thomas Barthalomew, Application for Relief, May 14, 1881, Applications for Relief files, Archives, KSHS.

12. "Miss Barton's Tour," *Dallas* [Tex.] *Daily Herald*, February 2, 1887, 4; W. C. Holden, "West Texas Drouths," *Southwestern Historical Quarterly* 32 (October 1928), 110–120; Sam S. Kepfield, "'They Were in Far Too Great Want': Federal Drought Relief to the Great Plains, 1887–1895," *South Dakota History* 28 (Winter 1998), 244–270; J. A. Munro, "Grasshopper Outbreaks in North Dakota, 1808–1948," *North Dakota History* 16 (July 1949), 144–248; "Interview with Mrs. R. D. Neal," 429, vol. 7, IP, Oklahoma; MacGinitie, *Not So Gay Nineties*, 130.

13. Colin Brummitt Goodykoontz, *Home Missions on the American Frontier* (Caldwell, Idaho: Caxton Printers, 1939), 333, quoting G. S. Codington in *Home Missionary* 47 (1874), 139; Ebbutt, *Emigrant Life in Kansas*, 129; Richmond, *Kansas, A Land of Contrasts*, 133, 134.

14. Robert N. Manley, "In the Wake of the Grasshoppers: Public Relief in Nebraska, 1874–1875," *Nebraska History* 44 (December 1963), 273; Dueker, "Pioneering on Snake Creek," in *Pioneer Tales of the North Platte Valley*, 82–86; Myrtle D. Fesler, *Pioneers of Western Kansas* (New York: Carlton Press, 1962), 13. Newspapers and state documents provide extensive information on relief efforts; for one example, see Nebraska Relief and Aid Society, Correspondence, 1875, file 1, box 1, Nebraska Relief and Aid Association, MS, NSHS.

15. *Review*, Coldwater, Kans., September 17, 1885; Glen Schwendemann, "Nicodemus: Negro Haven on the Solomon," *Kansas Historical Quarterly*, 34 (Spring 1968), 18; Holden, "West Texas Drouths," 112; Gilbert C. Fite, *The Farmers' Frontier, 1865–1900* (New York: Holt, Rinehart and Winston, 1966), 129–131; Mari Sandoz, *Old Jules* (New York: Blue Ribbon Books, 1935; reprint, Lincoln: University of Nebraska Press, 1962), 152; Nelson, "The First Hundred Years Are the Hardest," 8; "Kansas Land," Music file, Library, KSHS.

16. Hamlin Garland, *A Daughter of the Middle Border* (New York: Macmillan, 1921), ix, xi.

17. Hampsten, *Settlers' Children*, 31–34; Pabst, *Kansas Heritage*, 12, 15; "Pioneer Days of James Walter and Lydia Alice Germann (As remembered by their children)," in *Prairie Pioneers of Western Kansas and Eastern Colorado*, 54; Driscoll, *Kansas Irish*, 221–222; Miner, *West of Wichita*, 237; Liahna Babener, "Bitter Nostalgia: Recollections of Childhood on the Midwestern Frontier," in *Small Worlds: Children & Adolescents in America, 1850–1950*, eds. Elliott West and Paula Petrik (Lawrence: University of Kansas Press, 1992), 301–302.

18. Siceloff, *Boy Settler*, 184–185; Lewis, *Tapadero*, 69; Edith Eudora Kohl, *Land of the Burnt Thigh* (1938; reprint, St. Paul: Minnesota Historical Society Press, 1986), xxv; "A Letter from Out West," *Sentinel*, Harper, Kans., November 28, 1889; Robinson, *History of North Dakota*, 171; Thompson, "Pioneering on the Nebraska Prairies," 3, MS, NSHS.

19. Isabella L. Bird, *A Lady's Life in the Rocky Mountains* (Norman: University of Oklahoma Press, 1960), 47–48, 67; West, *Growing Up with the Country*, 147–149; Charles Alexander Eastman (Ohiyesa), *Indian Boyhood* (Boston: Little, Brown, 1902; reprint, Lincoln: University of Nebraska Press, 1991), 49; Margaret Connell Szasz, "Native American Children," in *American Childhood: A Research Guide and Historical Handbook*, eds. Joseph M. Hawes and N. Ray Hiner (Westport, Conn.: Greenwood Press, 1985), 318–320, 326.

20. Marilyn Irvin Holt, *The Orphan Trains: Placing Out in America* (Lincoln: University of Nebraska Press, 1992), 76; Bernard Wishy, *The Child and the Republic* (Philadelphia: University of Pennsylvania Press, 1968), 81–82.

21. Merrill J. Mattes, *Indians, Infants and Infantry: Andrew and Elizabeth Burt on the Frontier* (Denver: Old West Publishing Co., 1960; reprint, Lincoln: University of Nebraska Press, 1988), 7, 105, 121–122; Lydia Spencer Lane, *I Married a Soldier, or Old Days in the Old Army* (Philadelphia: J. B. Lippincott, 1893), 30–31; Agnes Wright Spring, *Cheyenne and Black Hills Stage and Express Routes* (Lincoln: University of Nebraska Press, 1948), 193–195.

22. Haywood, *Victorian West*, 155–156; Driscoll, *Kansas Irish*, 131, 335–336.

23. Sandoz, *Old Jules*, 5.

24. Thos. C. Wilson, "The Divorce Peril and Its Remedy," *Kansas Magazine* 1 (February 1909), 21–26; "Too Easy to Obtain Divorce in Kansas," *Mail and Breeze*, Topeka, July 21, 1899, and "Kansas Marriage Laws Have Followed Liberal Tradition of Pioneer Days," *Kansas City* [Mo.] *Star*, February 24, 1947, Divorce clipping file, Library, KSHS. See also Glenda Riley, *Divorce: An American Tradition* (New York: Oxford University Press, 1991; reprint, Lincoln: University of Nebraska Press, 1997); Theodore D. Woolsey, *Essay on Divorce and Divorce Legislation with Special Reference to the United States* (New York: Charles Scribner, 1969); Robert Griswold, "Law, Sex, Cruelty, and Divorce in Victorian America, 1840–1900," *American Quarterly* 38 (Winter 1986), 721–745; Lyn Ellen Bennett, "Reassessing Western Liberality: Divorce in Douglas County, Kansas, 1867–1876," *Kansas History* 17 (Winter 1994–1995), 274–87.

25. Wilson, "The Divorce Peril and Its Remedy," 24; Paula Petrik, "'If She Be Content': The Development of Montana Divorce Law, 1865–1907," *Western Historical Quarterly* 18 (July 1987), 264–265, 279, 290–291.

26. Cheyenne County and Lincoln County, Nebr. and Decatur County and Lane County, Kans., 1880 U.S. Census.

27. Fesler, *Pioneers of Western Kansas*, 86–87; John Talcott Norton Diary, May 7, 1878, MS, KSHS. For an overview of eastern placements in the West, see Holt, *Orphan Trains*.

28. Winifred N. Slagg, *Riley County Kansas* (Brooklyn, N.Y.: Theo Gaus' Sons, 1986), 223–224; *First Biennial Report of the Soldiers' Orphans' Home at Atchison, Kansas* (Topeka: Kansas Publishing House, 1888), 4; James C. Baccus, "'Your Gift Is Their Tomorrow': A History of the North Dakota Children's Home Society (Now Children's Village, Fargo, North Dakota)," *North Dakota History* 32 (January 1965), 139–142, 145; "The Masonic Home and School of Texas (The Masonic Orphans' Home)," 15–21, pamphlet (1919), and "In Memory of Colonel R. M. Wynne," 2–4, 6–7, pamphlet (ca. 1912), and Texas Research League, "The Child Care Program of the Texas State Orphans' Home at Cor-

sicana, Texas," 2, Interim Report, May 10, 1954, Library, Center for American History, University of Texas at Austin (hereinafter cited as Center for American History).

29. Porter, " 'Holding Down' a Northwest Kansas Claim," 224, 228.

30. Decatur County, Lane County, and Sheridan County, Kans., 1880 U S. Census.

31. Ibid. In 1900 approximately one of every four widows was under the age of forty-five; in 1956 the corresponding figure was one of twelve. See "Workshops 21–22—The Effect of the 'Affluent Society,' " 3, information sheet, 1960, box 119, folder 14, White House Conferences, DDE.

32. Robber's Roost Historical Society, *Pioneering on the Cheyenne River*, 68; Riley, "Journal of Carrie Robbins," 145; Michael B. Katz, *In the Shadow of the Poorhouse: A Social History of Welfare in America* (New York: Basic Books, 1986), 119; Shields, "Army Life on the Wyoming Frontier," 335.

33. "Christmas on the Frio (Mrs. Claudia Hobbs Davis)," in *Oldtimers of Southwest Texas*, comp. Florence Fenley (Uvalde, Tex.: Hornby Press, 1957), 47–48; "Cyrus B. 'Cy' Hagadone," in *Early and Modern History of Cozad [Nebraska] and Surrounding Community*, comp. Charles E. Allen (n.p., n.d.), 48; Kennon, *From the Pecos to the Powder*, 18, 20, 25–26.

Chapter 4. Education and School Building

1. "George White Family," in *Sod House Memories*, ed. Frances Jacobs Alberts (editor, 1972), 69.

2 Ewell, *Ten Years of My Life*, 26; Matthews, *Interwoven: A Pioneer Chronicle*, 50–51; Laurence, *Daughter of the Regiment*, 71, 92; Stallard, *Glittering Misery*, 94, 98.

3. Laurence, *Daughter of the Regiment*, 71; Martha Summerhayes, *Vanished Arizona: Recollections of the Army Life of a New England Woman* (Glorieta, N.M.: Rio Grande Press, 1970), 261; "Mrs. T. A. Arnold Interview," 464, vol. 12, IP, Oklahoma; "Mrs. S. S. Button," *Jetmore* [Kans.] *Republican*, April 25, 1930, 1; Stratton, *Pioneer Women*, 158; Cox, "Reflections of Early Days in Saline County," 32, MS, NSHS.

4. Stratton, *Pioneer Women*, 158; Lawrence W. Levine, *Highbrow/Lowbrow: The Emergence of Cultural Hierarchy in America* (Cambridge, Mass.: Harvard University Press, 1988), 17–18.

5. Driscoll, *Kansas Irish*, 139; Luna Warner, "The Diary of Luna E. Warner, A

Kansas Teenager of the Early 1870s," ed. Venola Lewis Bivens, *Kansas Historical Quarterly* 35 (Autumn 1969), 304; Laurence, *Daughter of the Regiment*, 71; Johnson, *William Allen White*, 20.

6. "Editor's Table," *Godey's Magazine and Lady's Book* 37 (July 1848), 52; "Editor's Table," *Godey's Magazine and Lady's Book* 41 (February 1854), 98; "Editor's Table," *Godey's Magazine and Lady's Book* 76 (March 1868), 243; Child, *The Mother's Book*, 93; Daniel T. Rodgers, "Socializing Middle-Class Children: Institutions, Fables, and Work Values in Nineteenth-Century America," in *American Childhood*, 128.

7. Sam Lewis Doughty to Alfred Humphrey, June 12, 1883, Humphrey Family Papers, Archives, South Dakota Historical Society, Pierre (hereinafter cited as SDHS); Driscoll, *Kansas Irish*, 139, 141; O'Kieffe, *Western Story*, xiv, 5.

8. "Mrs. S. S. Button," *Jetmore* [Kans.] *Republican*, April 25, 1930, 1; Lowe, "Growing Up in Kansas," 46; Martha Farnsworth Diary, January 2, 5, 9, 16, 19, 23, February 6, 16, 1883, MS, KSHS.

9. Edward Everett Dale, *Frontier Ways: Sketches of Life in the Old West* (Austin: University of Texas Press, 1959), 173–175, 185; O'Kieffe, *Western Story*, 70; Cox, "Reflections of Early Days in Saline County," 38, MS, NSHS; Henry Wylie Norton Diary, January 28, February 16, March 2, 6, April 10, 1885, MS, KSHS; West, *Growing Up with the Country*, 184–185.

10. Levine, *Highbrow/Lowbrow*, 26–27; Driscoll, *Kansas Irish*, 75–79.

11. MacGinitie, *Not So Gay Nineties*, 144; Dew M. Wisdom, U.S. Indian Agent, "Report of Union Agency," in *Annual Report of the Department of the Interior, Doc. No. 5, 55th Cong., 2d. sess.* (Washington, D.C.: Government Printing Office, 1897), 140; Miller, *The Dakotans*, 130.

12. Cox, "Reflections of Early Days in Saline County," 31, MS, NSHS; Kansas Preservation Dept., *Kansas Preservation Plan*, 57. State-supported universities were not funded or opened until statehood.

13. Ovella Dunn to Annie Moore, November 13, 1869; October 21, 1870, MS, KSHS; Dean, "Pioneering in Nebraska," 120, 121; Katie H. Armitage, "Elizabeth 'Bettie' Duncan: Diary of Daily Life, 1864," *Kansas History* 10 (Winter 1987–1988), 283; Mattes, *Indians, Infants and Infantry*, 233.

14. Charles Leslie Glenn, Jr., *The Myth of the Common School* (Amherst: University of Massachusetts Press, 1988), 78–81, 88–97, 263.

15. Wiebe, *They Seek a Country*, 125–126, 182; O'Kieffe, *Western Story*, 65; MacGinitie, *Not So Gay Nineties*, 185; Driscoll, *Kansas Irish*, 237.

16. Slagg, *Riley County Kansas*, 231; Hampsten, *Settlers' Children*, 70–71; "Daughters of Dakota," *South Dakota Report and Historical Collections* 33 (1966), 125;

Mary Hurlbut Cordier, *Schoolwomen of the Prairies and Plains: Personal Narratives from Iowa, Kansas, and Nebraska, 1860s–1920s* (Albuquerque: University of New Mexico Press, 1991), 117.

17. O'Kieffe, *Western Story*, 180; Dwight D. Eisenhower, *At Ease: Stories I Tell My Friends* (Garden City, N.Y.: Doubleday, 1967), 81; Horatio Alger, Jr., *Bound to Rise; or, Harry Walton's Motto* (Philadelphia: John C. Winston Co., 1873).

18. Cox, "Reflections of Early Days in Saline County," 31, 32, MS, NSHS; Dale, *Frontier Ways*, 156–157; Lulu Craig, "History of Nicodemus Colony," 39–40, Lulu Craig Papers, file 3, Kansas Collection.

19. *Manhattan* [Kans.] *Enterprise*, August 22, 1879; *Mercury*, Manhattan, Kans., June 16, September 15, 1886; James C. Carper, "The Popular Ideology of Segregated Schooling: Attitudes Toward the Education of Blacks in Kansas, 1854–1900," *Kansas History* 1 (Winter 1978), 262–263; Tim Gammon, "The Black Freedmen of the Cherokee Nation," *Negro History Bulletin* 40 (May–June 1977), 732–735; "Report of the Commissioner of Indian Affairs," in *Annual Reports of the Department of the Interior: Indian Affairs, Part I, Doc. No. 5, 57th Cong., 2d sess.* (Washington, D.C.: Government Printing Office, 1903), 130–131; William Loren Katz, *The Black West: A Documentary and Pictorial History of the African American Role in the Western Expansion of the United States* (New York: Simon & Schuster, 1996), chap. 9; Nell Irvin Painter, *Exodusters: Black Migration to Kansas After Reconstruction* (New York: Alfred A. Knopf, 1976), 46–47; Philip R. Beard, "The Kansas Colored Literary and Business Academy: A White Effort at African American Education in Late-Nineteenth-Century Kansas," *Kansas History* 24 (Autumn 2001), 200, 208.

20. Kenneth A. Stern and Janelle L. Wagner, "The First Decade of Educational Governance in Kansas, 1855–1865," *Kansas History* 24 (Spring 2001), 40, 53; Gladys McArdle, "An 1876 Model Kansas School," 1, Native Sons and Daughters of Kansas Collection, MS, KSHS; O'Kieffe, *Western Story*, 180; Dale, *Frontier Ways*, 156–157; Cordier, *Schoolwomen*, 51–55.

21. Cox, "Reflections of Early Days in Saline County," 34, MS, NSHS; Sam Lewis Doughty to Alfred Humphrey, June 12, 1883, February 21, April 13, 1884, SDHS.

22. Emma Pospisil, "A Teacher of the Willow Creek School," *Nebraska History* 24 (January–February 1943), 18.

23. Porter, "Catherine Emma Wiggins," 18–20; Ise, *Sod and Stubble*, 235; MacGinitie, *Not So Gay Nineties*, 139.

24. Laurence, *Daughter of the Regiment*, 74, 89; Driscoll, *Kansas Irish*, 309; Burdick, "Recollections of Graham's Island," 10.

25. Cox, "Reflections of Early Days in Saline County," 34, MS, NSHS; Summerhayes, *Vanished Arizona*, 261; Stallard, *Glittering Misery*, 94–95; Porter, "Catherine Emma Wiggins," 19.

26. Elizabeth Pleck, *Domestic Tyranny: The Making of Social Policy Against Family Violence from Colonial Times to the Present* (New York: Oxford University Press, 1987), 78; Wishy, *The Child and the Republic*, 45; Brown, "Tendency of Punishments," 84; "Home Training of Children," *Monthly Religious Magazine* 10 (January 1853), 24; "Little Children," *Godey's Magazine and Lady's Book* 48 (March 1854), 207.

27. Laurence, *Daughter of the Regiment*, xxvii, 17; Robber's Roost Historical Society, *Pioneering on the Cheyenne River*, 45; O'Kieffe, *Western Story*, 6; Dean, "Pioneering in Nebraska," 113–114; West, *Growing Up with the Country*, 158–160.

28. "Vera Best Interview," vol. 15, 83, IP, Oklahoma; McArdle, "An 1876 Model Kansas School," 1, MS, KSHS; Armitage, "Elizabeth 'Bettie' Duncan," 279, 283, 285; O'Kieffe, *Western Story*, 64–65; Kennon, *From the Pecos to the Powder*, 16–17; Stratton, *Pioneer Women*, 165.

29. "Daughters of Dakota," 133; Alice R. Lacey, ed., *South Dakota's American Mother: The Life Story of Christina K. Lacey, South Dakota's State Mother, 1946* (Sioux Falls, S.D.: Pheasant Press, 1989), 25–26; Martha Farnsworth Diary, January 26, November 10, 1883, MS, KSHS.

30. Mary W. M. Hargreaves, "Rural Education on the Northern Plains Frontier," *Journal of the West* 18 (October 1979), 25; John Talcott Norton Diary, April 28, 1878, MS, KSHS; *Albany* [Tex.] *Echo*, June 9, 1883, 2; "Pioneer Days of James Walter," in *Prairie Pioneers of Western Kansas and Eastern Colorado*, 52.

31. West, *Growing Up with the Country*, 190, citing U.S. Census, 1870, and U.S. Census, 1880; Cordier, *Schoolwomen*, 23; *Second Biennial Report of the Kansas State Board of Education* (Topeka: George W. Martin, Kansas Publishing House, 1880), 384–385.

32. Wayne E. Fuller, *The Old Country School: The Story of Rural Education in the Middle West* (Chicago: University of Chicago Press, 1988), 240–241; Cordier, *Schoolwomen*, 51–52; Clyde Lyndon King, "The Kansas School System—Its History and Tendencies," *Kansas Historical Collections* 11 (1909–1910), 424–455; Hargreaves, "Rural Education on the Northern Plains Frontier," 29.

33. Cordier, *Schoolwomen*, 110; Cox, "Reflections of Early Days in Saline County," 36, MS, NSHS.

Chapter 5. The Work of Children

1. Siceloff, *Boy Settler*, 99; "Children in the Garden," *Tilton's Journal of Horticulture and Florist's Companion* 6 (September 1869), 151.
2. For one treatment of the subject, see Viviana A. Zelizer, *Pricing the Priceless Child: The Changing Social Value of Children* (New York: Basic Books, 1985), particularly chap. 2.
3. Eisenhower, *At Ease*, 70, 73; Edward S. "Ned" Beck Diary, June 28, July 15, 24, August 7, 26, 27, 28, 1880, MS, KSHS; Della Knowles Diary, 1892, Kansas Collection; "Lawrence D. Adams Interview," 84–85, vol. 12, IP, Oklahoma; Robber's Roost Historical Society, *Pioneering on the Cheyenne River*, 40; Ewell, *Ten Years of My Life*, 34; Pabst, *Kansas Heritage*, 101; Lowe, "Growing Up in Kansas," 40.
4. Mari Sandoz, *Old Jules Country: A Selection from the Works of Mari Sandoz* (New York: Hastings House, 1965), 303.
5. Curtis Hoppin Norton Diary, February 8, 1878, MS, KSHS; "C. F. (Bud) Jones of Sabinal," 141, and "Mrs. Mary Elizabeth Vaughn Winn, 100 Year Old Mother," 12, in *Oldtimers of Southwest Texas*; MacGinitie, *Not So Gay Nineties*, 12–21; Pabst, *Kansas Heritage*, 125–126. For one literary reference to immigrant women, see Willa Cather, *My Ántonia*, in *Willa Cather: Early Novels and Stories* (New York: Penguin Putnam, 1987), 794, 810, 825.
6. Singley, "A Pioneer Family," in *Pioneer Stories of Meade County*, 215; Everett Dick, *Conquering the Great American Desert: Nebraska* (Lincoln: Nebraska State Historical Society, 1975), 58–59; Robert C. Haywood, "Sod, Straw, and Sunflower Stalks: The Homestead Act and Jefferson's Yeoman Farmers in Kansas and Nebraska," *Prairie Scout* (1985), 147–148.
7. Deborah J. Hoskins, "Brought, Bought, and Borrowed: Material Culture on the Oklahoma Farming Frontier, 1889–1907," in *At Home on the Range: Essays on the History of Western and Social Life*, ed. John R. Wunder (Westport, Conn.: Greenwood Press, 1985), 124; *Sentinel*, Harper, Kans., November 28, 1889, 2; Ebbutt, *Emigrant Life in Kansas*, 17–18.
8. "Memories of Agnes Krom Quick," in *Dodge City Pioneer Stories*, 77; Pabst, *Kansas Heritage*, 15; "Daughters of Dakota," 138; MacGinitie, *Not So Gay*

Nineties, 113; Stanley, "Prairie Home Companions," 16–17; Siceloff, *Boy Settler*, 100.

9. O'Kieffe, *Western Story*, 37; MacGinitie, *Not So Gay Nineties*, 113; Cox, "Reflections of Early Days in Saline County," 28–29, MS, NSHS; Porter, "'Holding Down' a Northwest Kansas Claim," 231; "Harvey Benson," in *Oldtimers of Southwest Texas*, 105.

10. Miller, *The Dakotans*, 108; Driscoll, *Kansas Irish*, 107–111; Lowe, "Growing Up in Kansas," 42.

11. Lowe, "Growing Up in Kansas," 43.

12. Driscoll, *Kansas Irish*, 172; "The Everett E. Harrington Story," in *Prairie Pioneers*, 59. For two discussions on butter production, see "Butter Making and Economic Development in Mid-Atlantic America, 1750–1850," 170–185, and "Cloth, Butter, and Boarders: Women's Household Production for Market," 186–205, in Joan M. Jensen, *Promise to the Land: Essays on Rural Women* (Albuquerque: University of New Mexico Press, 1991).

13. Kennon, *From the Pecos to the Powder*, 20; Robber's Roost Historical Society, *Pioneering on the Cheyenne River*, 45–46; Miller, *The Dakotans*, 108; Dean, "Pioneering in Nebraska," 119.

14. Decatur County, Kans., Lane County, Kans., and Cheyenne County, Nebr., 1880 U.S. Census; Robber's Roost Historical Society, *Pioneering on the Cheyenne River*, 68, 92; Lewis, *Tapadero*, 51, 53, 74–75, 79.

15. Roosa, "Homesteading in the 1880's," 377; Laurence, *Daughter of the Regiment*, 24; Ligon, *Just Dad*, 23–24; Robber's Roost Historical Society, *Pioneering on the Cheyenne River*, 23, 45.

16. Jesse Brown and A. M. Willard, *The Black Hills Trail: A History of the Struggles of the Pioneers in the Winning of the Black Hills* (Rapid City, S.D.: Rapid City Journal Co.; reprint, New York: Arno Press, 1975), 522; MacGinitie, *Not So Gay Nineties*, 24–25; DeWitt Clinton Grinell Diary, July 5, August 8, September 16, October 1, 18, 1867, MS, KSHS.

17. *Daily Pantagraph*, Bloomington, Ill., January 5, 1858; Olive Capper Diary, 1895, MS, KSHS; H. E. Stears to Governor John P. St. John, August 9, 1879, Governor St. John Correspondence, box 14, folder 5, Archives, KSHS; Haywood, "Hodgeman County Colony," 217, 220; Cather, *My Ántonia*, in *Willa Cather: Early Novels and Stories*, 839.

18. Russell, "Julia Cody Goodman," 475–476; Mattes, *Indians, Infants and Infantry*, 97, 179.

19. Holt, *Orphan Trains*, chap. 2; *Union*, Junction City, Kans., December 11,

1869. *Frank Leslie's Illustrated Newspaper*, December 25, 1869, carried an illustration of boys arriving from London's Home and Refuge for Destitute Children.

20. David J. Rothman, *The Discovery of the Asylum: Social Order and Disorder in the New Republic* (Boston: Little, Brown, 1971), 185; Holt, *Orphan Trains*, 43–44, 89–90, 178–179; Neva R. Deardorff, "Bound Out," *Survey* 56 (July 15, 1926), 459; "Indentured Children," *School and Society* 26 (November 26, 1927), 674; "Editorial," *Dallas* [Tex.] *Daily Herald*, February 22, 1887, 4.

21. Cox, "Reflections of Early Days in Saline County," 40, MS, NSHS; Lowe, "Growing Up in Kansas," 45–46; *Lane County Gazette*, California, Kans., February 26, 1880; Stanley, *Cowboy Josh*, 28; Johnson, *Happy as a Big Sunflower*, 36; John Talcott Norton Diary, January 26, February 15, 1878, MS, KSHS; O'Kieffe, *Western Story*, 26–27. For an overview of the Dakota bone trade, see Le Roy Barnett, "The Buffalo Bone Commerce on the Northern Plains," *North Dakota History* 39 (Winter 1972), 23–42.

22. "Rawlins County," *Attwood* [Kans.] *Pioneer*, October 23, 1879, 1; Stanley, *Cowboy Josh*, 37–38; "Arthur Wilson and Lydia Pottorff Adams," in *Dodge City Pioneer Stories*, 88.

23. Lowe, "Growing Up in Kansas," 51; Wentz family, Decatur County, Kans., 1880 U.S. Census; Pabst, *Kansas Heritage*, 24–25; Hampsten, *Settlers' Children*, 71.

24. " 'As a Twig Is Bent': Childhood in Texas, 1800–1900," *Star of the Republic Museum Notes* 12 (Winter 1987), 2, newsletter, Childhood vertical file, Center for American History; L. O. McHenry, "Historical Reminiscence by Native Son of Valley," in *Pioneer Tales of the North Platte Valley and Nebraska Panhandle*, 55; Lacey, *South Dakota's American Mother*, 21; Siceloff, *Boy Settler*, 38–39, 40–41.

25. Bird, *Lady's Life in the Rocky Mountains*, 67.

26. West, *Growing Up with the Country*, 252–254.

Chapter 6. Play and Leisure

1. John Talcott Norton Diary, May 6, July 1, 1877; February 14, 1878, and Curtis Hoppin Norton Diary, February 27, 1878, MS, KSHS; Dean, "Pioneering in Nebraska," 113.

2. Ewell, *Ten Years of My Life*, 10; Kennon, *From the Pecos to the Powder*, 21;

MacGinitie, *Not So Gay Nineties*, 93, 183; Ebbutt, *Emigrant Life in Kansas*, 34–35.

3. Bernard Mergen, "Made, Bought, and Stolen: Toys and the Culture of Childhood," in *Small Worlds*, 88; Siceloff, *Boy Settler*, 189–190.

4. Mattes, *Indians, Infants and Infantry*, 143; MacGinitie, *Not So Gay Nineties*, 75; Thompson, "Pioneering on the Nebraska Prairies," 4, MS, NSHS.

5. Miriam Formanek-Brunell, "Sugar and Spite: The Politics of Doll Play in Nineteenth-Century America," in *Small Worlds*, 113; MacGinitie, *Not So Gay Nineties*, 75.

6. Formanek-Brunell, "Sugar and Spite," in *Small Worlds*, 107–109, 113, 117; MacGinitie, *Not So Gay Nineties*, 87–88.

7. For *Godey's* and other publications, see Marilyn Irvin, "The Cult of Childhood in Nineteenth-Century America," 14–15, master's thesis, University of Illinois–Springfield, 1981.

8. Carroll Smith-Rosenberg, *Disorderly Conduct: Visions of Gender in Victorian America* (New York: Aflred A. Knopf, 1985), 61; Formanek-Burnell, "Sugar and Spite," in *Small Worlds*, 116; Ovella Dunn to Annie Moore, December 3, 1869, MS, KSHS; Driscoll, *Kansas Irish*, 235.

9. West, *Growing Up with the Country*, 114, quoting from Augusta Dodge Thomas, "Prairie Children," 58–59, MS, KSHS; Formanek-Brunell, "Sugar and Spite," in *Small Worlds*, 117, 121–123; A. C. Ellis and G. Stanley Hall, "Study of Dolls," *Pedagogical Seminary* 1 (December 1896), 146.

10. MacGinitie, *Not So Gay Nineties*, 105; Sandoz, *Love Song to the Plains*, 67–68; Driscoll, *Kansas Irish*, 87–89.

11. John Talcott Norton Diary, May–November 1877; February 4, 1878, MS, KSHS; MacGinitie, *Not So Gay Nineties*, 219; Kennon, *From the Pecos to the Powder*, 8–9; Stallard, *Glittering Misery*, 80–81; Walker, "Old Fort Berthold," 36–37.

12. Westergaard, "History of the Danish Settlement," 161; Stallard, *Glittering Misery*, 83; Martha Farnsworth Diary, January 25, 1883, MS, KSHS.

13. Laurence, *Daughter of the Regiment*, 74, 97; "Hints About Children," *Godey's Magazine and Lady's Book* 64 (August 1862), 198; Beekman, *Mechanical Baby*, 109–112; Dominick J. Cavallo, "Social Reform and the Movement to Organize Children's Play During the Progressive Era," *History of Childhood Quarterly* 3 (1976), 509, 513; Haywood and Jarvis, *"Funnie Place, No Fences,"* 20.

14. West, *Growing Up with the Country*, 111–112; Della Knowles Diary, July 11, 1892, Kansas Collection.

15. John Greenway, ed., *Folklore of the Great West* (Palo Alto, Calif.: American West Publishing Co., 1969), 425–431; Dale, *Frontier Ways*, 141; Ebbutt, *Emigrant Life in Kansas*, 57; Driscoll, *Kansas Irish*, 251–252.

16. Dale, *Frontier Ways*, 141; DeWitt Clinton Grinell Diary, December 30, 1868, MS, KSHS; Lowe, "Growing Up in Kansas," 50.

17. Driscoll, *Kansas Irish*, 259; MacGinitie, *Not So Gay Nineties*, 223; Martha Farnsworth Diary, February 27, 1883, MS, KSHS; Cox, "Reflections of Early Days in Saline County," 36–37, MS, NSHS; Della Knowles Diary, November 9, 1892, Kansas Collection.

18. Willa Cather, "The Incomparable Opera House," ed. Mildred R. Bennett, *Nebraska History* 49 (Winter 1968), 373–375; Della Knowles Diary, November 11, 1892, Kansas Collection; Levine, *Highbrow/Lowbrow*, 7–8, 221–225.

19. Pabst, *Kansas Heritage*, 138–139; Roosa, "Homesteading in the 1880's," 382; Laurence, *Daughter of the Regiment*, 74.

20. *The Cowboy*, Sidney, Kans., September 29, 1883, 2; David Murphy, "Dramatic Expressions: Czech Theatre Curtains in Nebraska," *Nebraska History* 74 (Fall-Winter 1993), 172; Eisenhower, *At Ease*, 68.

21. U.S. Department of the Interior, *Promised Land on the Solomon*, 66; "Emancipation Day," *Nationalist*, Manhattan, Kans., August 5, 1880; Richmond, *Kansas, A Land of Contrasts*, 153; Tommy R. Thompson, "Wearin' of the Green: The Irish and Saint Patrick's Day in Omaha," *Nebraska History* 81 (Winter 2000), 170–178; "Germans Enjoying High Life," *Abilene* [Kans.] *Daily Reflector*, September 21, 1898, 3.

22. Westergaard, "History of Danish Settlement," 161; John Talcott Norton Diary, October 1, 1877, and DeWitt Clinton Grinell Diary, May 26, 1867, MS, KSHS.

23. Ovella Dunn to Annie Moore, November 26, 1870; DeWitt Clinton Grinell Diary, April 21, 1867, and July 4, 1868; and Henry Wylie Norton Diary, April 5, 1885, MS, KSHS; Elizabeth M. Yerina, "Christmas and Other Traditional Holidays of the Germans on the Volga," trans. Richard Rye, *Journal of the American Historical Society of Germans from Russia* 21 (Fall 1998), 10; Cora Dolbee, "The Fourth of July in Early Kansas, 1854–1857," *Kansas Historical Quarterly* 10 (1941), 38; "Mrs. T. A. Arnold Interview," 464, vol. 12, IP, Oklahoma; Della Knowles Diary, July 4, 1892, Kansas Collection; MacGinitie, *Not So Gay Nineties*, 226–227; J. D. McKelvey to the Board of Public Lands and Buildings, August 1, 1893, Girls' Training School, file 1, subgroup 3, Department of Public Institutions, MS, NSHS.

24. "Vera Best Interview," vol. 15, 83, IP, Oklahoma; Henry Wylie Norton Diary, December 24, 25, 1884, MS, KSHS; Mrs. J. W. Edwards, "Pioneer Family

Life—Edward H. Bayer," in *Pioneer Stories of Meade County*, 27; Lowe, "Growing Up in Kansas," 51.

25. Fr. John B. Terbovich, "Religious Folklore Among the German-Russians in Ellis County, Kansas," *Western Folklore* 22 (April 1963), 85; Yerina, "Christmas and Other Traditional Holidays," 7–8; Ovella Dunn to Annie Moore, December 18, 1869, MS, KSHS; "Christmas Tree," *Chronicle*, Abilene, Kans., November 30, 1871, 2; MacGinitie, *Not So Gay Nineties*, 217–218. For an overview of some traditions, see Daniel B. Nystrom, *Scandinavian Christmas Traditions* (Apple Valley, Minn: Twin Rainbow Press, 1987).

26. Laurence, *Daughter of the Regiment*, 27–29; Mattes, *Indians, Infants and Infantry*, 143.

Chapter 7. Matters of Life and Death

1. Laura Ingalls Wilder, *The Long Winter* (New York: Harper & Brothers, 1940), 37, 45, 62.

2. Stanley, *Cowboy Josh*, 89–90, 146; Cox, "Reflections of Early Days in Saline County," 43, MS, NSHS; Dean, "Pioneering in Nebraska," 110.

3. Lon Ford, *"The Kid": Lon Ford Story*, ed. Bonnie Ford Swayze (Ashland, Kans.: Clipperprint, 1982), 10; O. P. Byers, "Personal Recollections of the Terrible Blizzard of 1886," *Kansas Historical Quarterly* 12 (1911–1912), 101.

4. Byers, "Personal Recollections," 115–116, citing *Western Kansas World*, WaKeeney, Kans., January 23, 1886.

5. "The Blizzard in the Northwest," *Frank Leslie's Illustrated Newspaper* 65 (January 28, 1888), 398–399; "Diary of a Swedish Immigrant, 1888–1899," 2, translated copy, John Alfred Borg file, MS, NSHS; "Minnie Mae Freeman," newspaper clipping, Minnie Mae Freeman file, MS, NSHS; Sandoz, *Love Song to the Plains*, 140–141. A large number of accounts appear in W. H. O'Gara, comp., *In All Its Fury: A History of the Blizzard of January 12, 1888, With Stories and Reminiscences* (Lincoln, Nebr.: Blizzard Club, 1947; reprint, Lincoln: Doris Jenkins, 1973).

6. Ovella Dunn to Annie J. Moore, November 3, 1869, MS, KSHS; "Vera Best Interview," 83–84, vol. 15, IP, Oklahoma; Johnson, *William Allen White's America*, 21; "A Funnie Place, No Fences," in *"A Funnie Place, No Fences,"* 7–8; Dean, "Pioneering in Nebraska," 107; MacGinitie, *Not So Gay Nineties*, 26; Sandoz, *Love Song to the Plains*, 139.

7. "A Funnie Place, No Fences," in *"A Funnie Place, No Fences,"* 8; MacGinitie,

Not So Gay Nineties, 12, 182–183; Ellis, *Life of an Ordinary Woman*, 76; Schubert, *Buffalo Soldiers*, 58–59; Maude A. McFadin, *The John Stephen McFadin Family* (North Newton, Kans.: Mennonite Press, 1971), 75–76.

8. West, *Growing Up with the Country*, 221; Charles R. King, "Childhood Death: The Health Care of Children on the Kansas Frontier," *Kansas History* 14 (Spring 1991), 26; "Names of Persons Who Died in Dakota Territory During the Year Ending June, 1870," *South Dakota Historical Collections* 10 (1920), 440–442; Arthur E. Hertzler, *The Doctor and His Patients: The American Domestic Scene as Viewed by a Family Doctor* (New York: Harper & Brothers, 1940), 27. Dakota percentages reflect American-born and immigrant residents; five additional deaths, those of Indian or "half-Indian" children, were not included.

9. "What Came of It" and "Plucky Boy," *Dallas* [Tex.] *Daily Herald*, February 21, 1887, 2, 3; Ewell, *Ten Years of My Life*, 9; Work Projects Administration, Writer's Project, State of Kansas, *Lamps on the Prairie: A History of Nursing in Kansas* (Emporia, Kans.: Emporia Gazette Press, 1942), 54.

10. West, *Growing Up with the Country*, 219–220; Laurence, *Daughter of the Regiment*, 10; Ise, *Sod and Stubble*, 84–85; Mildred A. Renaud, "Rattlesnakes and Tumbleweed: A Memoir of South Dakota," *American Heritage* 26 (April 1975), 56; Elizabeth Hampsten, *Read This Only to Yourself: The Private Writings of Midwestern Women, 1880–1910* (Bloomington: University of Indiana Press, 1982), 47.

11. Barry, *Beginning of the West*, 206, 259, 260, 275, 293, 318, 341, 373, 443, 464, 536, 1060.

12. Ibid, 1060; Unruh, *The Plains Across*, 345–346; Natalie Morrison Denison, "Missions and Missionaries of the Presbyterian Church, U.S., Among the Choctaws—1866–1907," *Chronicles of Oklahoma* 24 (Winter 1946–1947), 433; J. D. McKelvey to John C. Allen, March 31, 1894, and J. D. McKelvey to J. A. Piper, February 26, and April 8, 1895, file 2, Girls' Training School, MS, NSHS.

13. Schubert, *Buffalo Soldiers*, 58; Stewart, "Army Laundresses," 422; Mattes, *Indians, Infants and Infantry*, 230–231.

14. Pabst, *Kansas Heritage*, 134; King, "Childhood Death," 32; "Save the Youngest: Seven Charts on Maternal and Infant Mortality, With Explanatory Comment," *Children's Bureau Publication No. 61* (1919), 9–11; Viola I. Paradise, "Maternity Care and the Welfare of Young Children in a Homesteading County in Montana," Rural Child Welfare Series No. 3, *Children's Bureau Publication No. 34* (1919), 23, 71, 75; Florence Brown Sherbon and

Elizabeth Moore, "Maternity and Infant Care in Two Rural Counties in Wisconsin," Rural Child Welfare Series No. 4, *Children's Bureau Publication No. 46* (1919), 53, 92; Hertzler, *The Doctor and His Patients*, 31–32.

15. Haywood, *Victorian West*, 82–83; "City Dads Meet," *Abilene* [Kans.] *Daily Reflector*, September 3, 1898, 3.

16. Crumbine, *Frontier Doctor*, 60.

17. "Pioneer Days of James Walter and Lydia Alice Germann," in *Prairie Pioneers of Western Kansas and Eastern Colorado*, 55.

18. William Warren Sweet, *Religion on the American Frontier, 1783–1840*, vol. 4, *The Methodists* (New York: Cooper Square Publishers, 1964), 508; Kansas State Board of Health, *First Annual Report, 1885* (Topeka: State Printer, 1886), 73–74, 90; Crumbine, *Frontier Doctor*, 60; Susan S. Novak, "Well Intentioned, Ill Advised," *Kansas Heritage* 10 (Spring 2002), 18.

19. Lowe, "Growing Up in Kansas," 48; West, *Growing Up with the Country*, 220–221; Singley, "A Pioneer Family," in *Pioneer Stories of Meade County*, 215; WPA, *Lamps on the Prairie*, 39.

20. Lowe, "Growing Up in Kansas," 48.

21. "Save the Youngest: Seven Charts on Maternal and Infant Mortality," 2, 5.

22. WPA, *Lamps on the Prairie*, 41–42; Dale, *Frontier Ways*, 200; DeWitt Clinton Grinell Diary, April 6, 8, August 8, 24, 1867, MS, KSHS.

23. Adelaide Hechtlinger, *The Great Patent Medicine Era, or Without Benefit of Doctor* (New York: Grosset & Dunlap, 1970), 122, 124; Crumbine, *Frontier Doctor*, 61.

24. Hechtlinger, *Great Patent Medicine Era*, 29; Dale, *Frontier Ways*, 194–195, 197–198; Martha Farnsworth Diary, March 15, 1883, MS, KSHS; Shirley Fischer Arends, *The Central Dakota Germans: Their History, Language, and Culture* (Washington, D.C.: Georgetown University Press, 1989), 196; Sanford, *Journal of Mollie Dorsey Sanford*, 49; Crumbine, *Frontier Doctor*, 127; WPA, *Lamps on the Prairie*, 39, 41; William E. Koch, *Folklore from Kansas: Customs, Beliefs, and Superstitions* (Lawrence: Regents Press of Kansas, 1980), 113, 133, 135; "Good for What Ails You—Wild Herbs," in *Bittersweet Earth*, ed. Ellen Gray Massey (Norman: University of Oklahoma Press, 1985), 303–324; Wayland D. Hand, "A Miscellany of Nebraska Folk Beliefs," *Western Folklore* 21 (October 1962), 260–262.

25. Dean, "Pioneering in Nebraska," 116–117.

26. Singley, "A Pioneer Family," in *Pioneer Stories of Meade County*, 215; Narcissa Owen, *Memoirs of Narcissa Owen, 1831–1907* (Siloam Springs, Ark.: Simon Sager Press and Siloam Springs Museum, 1983), 88–89; Arends, *Central*

Dakota Germans, 195; Driscoll, *Kansas Irish*, 64–67; WPA, *Lamps on the Prairie*, 39.

27. Miner, *West of Wichita*, 169; "A Funnie Place, No Fences," in *"A Funnie Place, No Fences,"* 12, 13; Hertzler, *The Doctor and His Patients*, 8, 9; Hampsten, *Settlers' Children*, 177–176.

28. "Pearlette," *Pearlette* [Kans.] *Call*, April 15, 1879, 1; "Meade County in 1879, Personal Recollection, by A. Bennett, for the Graphic," *Fowler City* [Kans.] *Graphic*, August 6, 1885, 2; Fesler, *Pioneers of Western Kansas*, 38; Lewis, *Tapadero*, 67; Ebbutt, *Emigrant Life in Kansas*, 211; *Wichita Beacon*, June 24, 1874, 2; Arends, *Central Dakota Germans*, 137–138, 142; Driscoll, *Kansas Irish*, 56.

29. Katherine G. Fougera, *With Custer's Cavalry: From the Memoirs of the Late Katherine Gibson* (Caldwell, Idaho: Caxton Printers, 1940), 254–256; McFadin, *The John Stephen McFadin Family*, 75–76; Roosa, "Homesteading in the 1880's," 386; "Meade County in 1879," *Fowler City Graphic*, August 6, 1885.

30. Arends, *Central Dakota Germans*, 142; Ellis, *Life of an Ordinary Woman*, 13; Driscoll, *Kansas Irish*, 56–57. For an excellent review of mourning dress, see Loren N. Horton, "In the Midst of Life: Victorian Funeral Etiquette," *Hope & Glory* 3 (Spring 1988), 48–61.

31. "A Strange Infanticide at Wilson," *Star-Sentinel*, Hays, Kans., July 9, 1885, 1.

32. Pabst, *Kansas Heritage*, 134; "Frank J. Best Interview," 73, vol. 15, IP, Oklahoma; William J. Ward and Margaret C. Ward, "Green-Wood and the Rural Cemetery Movement," *Hope & Glory* 1 (Spring 1987), 43–45; Stanley French, "The Cemetery as Cultural Institution: The Establishment of Mount Auburn and the Rural Cemetery Movement," in *Death in America*, ed. David E. Stannard (Philadelphia: University of Pennsylvania Press, 1975), 78.

33. DeWitt Clinton Grinell Diary, August 2, 1867, and Henry Wylie Norton Journal, April 5, 1884, MS, KSHS; "Composed by Miss Allie Pettus," in *"A Funnie Place, No Fences,"* 335; Laurence, *Daughter of the Regiment*, 9.

Chapter 8. Common Threads

1. Burdick, "Recollections of Graham's Island," 8–9.

2. Barry, *Beginning of the West*, 217, 281.

3. Porter, "'Holding Down' a Northwest Kansas Claim," 233; MacGinitie, *Not So Gay Nineties*, 109; Jack W. Heard, *The Pictorial Military Life History of Jack*

Whitehead Heard (San Antonio, Tex.: Schneider Printing Co., 1969), 4; Stanley, *Cowboy Josh*, 24–25; Cole, "Pioneer Life in Kansas," 353.

4. Johnson, *Happy as a Big Sunflower*, 15; Margaret Hill McCarter, *The Price of the Prairie: The Story of Kansas* (New York: A. L. Burt, 1912), 487–488; Loewen, *Hidden Worlds*, 65; O. E. Rölvaag, *Peder Victorious: A Tale of the Pioneers Twenty Years Later* (New York: Harper & Brothers, 1929; reprint, Lincoln: University of Nebraska Press, 1982), xii–xiii, xvii.

5. Sandoz, *Old Jules Country*, 303–304; "Mrs. M. O. Bezanson Interview," 94, vol. 15, IP, Oklahoma; Stratton, *Pioneer Women*, 60.

6. James B. Shortridge, "The Expectations of Others: Struggles Toward a Sense of Place in the Northern Plains," in *Many Wests: Place, Culture and Regional Identity*, eds. David M. Wrobel and Michael C. Steiner (Lawrence: University Press of Kansas, 1997), 120; Wright Morris, "How I Put in the Time," in *Growing Up Western*, ed. Clarus Backes (New York: HarperCollins Publishers, 1991), 110; Thompson, "Pioneering on the Nebraska Prairies," 4, MS, NSHS.

A Note on Sources

THE WORKING BIBLIOGRAPHY for this volume was developed within two broad categories. The first contained documentary evidence directly related to childhood experiences and memories. The second consisted of materials that informed the context of those experiences and memories. The disparate subjects within the second category were studied for relevancy to an event, historical interpretation, or local story. For example, a volume on the military frontier was a source for references to children and post life, not army campaigns or well-known leaders. The result was a diverse list of sources that ranged in subject, from Western expansion to railroads to folklore to social reform. In this essay I make no attempt to list all the materials I consulted, but I do note selected publications along with primary sources and collections.

The foundation for this study were diaries, journals, letters, autobiographies, and reminiscences that told the story of nineteenth-century plains life from the perspective of children and adolescents. Anyone working in these materials knows that the number of extant records is staggering. They can be found in state and local historical societies, college and university archives, and holdings of private organizations. A single collection may contain a few items, such as the Harriett Ovella Dunn Letters at the Kansas State Historical Society, or it may consist of larger sets of family materials, such as the Pichler Family and Humphrey Family collections at the South Dakota Historical Society. One of the largest single collections is the Oklahoma Historical Society's Indian-Pioneer Collection, compiled and indexed as a WPA project. Interviews and documentary materials from this collection are cited in the text, as are sources from the

Center for American History, University of Texas at Austin; Kansas Collection, University of Kansas, Lawrence; and the Dwight D. Eisenhower Presidential Library, Abilene, Kansas. Additionally, some collections relate only to a specific group. Among these, and not cited elsewhere, are the Germans from Russia Heritage Collection at the North Dakota Institute for Regional Studies, North Dakota State University, Fargo, and the Mennonite Library and Archives, Bethel College, North Newton, Kansas.

Beginning in the late 1800s, state and local societies actively collected diaries, letters, and journals of settlers and town builders. Families and individuals readily donated materials. There was a palpable sense that ordinary people had been part of something extraordinary in state and regional history and that their stories should be saved for the historical record. That feeling was reinforced during the 1930s when local newspapers published "old settler" stories to record the past and remind a younger generation that tough times were not new to the plains. The message suggested that the Great Depression and the Dust Bowl could be endured, just as pioneers had survived any number of earlier hardships.

Nineteenth-century newspapers provide excellent local accounts, and county histories are a useful source of information. Quality varies widely, but beyond predictable recitations of statistics and dates there are good firsthand accounts, family stories, and historical overviews of an area and its settlement. Among those consulted were *Pioneering on the Cheyenne River* (1947), compiled by Robber's Roost Historical Society, Lusk, Wyoming; *Big Sioux Pioneers: Essays About the Settlement of the Dakota Prairie Frontier* (1980), edited by Arthur R. Huseboe and published by the Norland Heritage Foundation; *Pioneer Stories of Meade County* (1965), compiled by the Meade County, Kansas, Council of Women's Clubs; *Prairie Pioneers of Western Kansas and Eastern Colorado* (1956) by John C. and Winoma C. Jones; *Pioneer Tales of the North Platte Valley and Nebraska Panhandle* (1938), compiled by A. B. Wood; and *Dodge City and Ford County, Kansas, Pioneer Histories and Stories, 1870–1920* (1996), compiled by the Ford County Historical Society.

State historical societies have traditionally published diaries, letters, and reminiscences in their journals. Among the more interesting and useful were Blanche Beal Lowe, "Growing Up in Kansas," *Kansas History* 8 (Spring 1985); Adelia Clifton, "A Pioneer Family in Old Greer County," *Chronicles of Oklahoma* 24 (Winter 1946–1947); Fannie E. Cole, "Pioneer Life in Kansas," *Kansas Historical Collections* 12 (1911–1912); Frank Dean, "Pioneering in Nebraska, 1872–1879," *Nebraska History* 36 (June 1955); and James F. Walker, "Old Fort Berthold as I Knew It," *North Dakota History* 20 (January 1953). There are many others, of course, but these voices spoke with memorable personalities.

The same can be said for a number of books. Among those used extensively were Charles B. Driscoll, *Kansas Irish* (New York: Macmillan, 1943); Clara E. Ewell, *Ten Years of My Life* (author, 1973); John Ise, *Sod and Stubble: The Story of a Kansas Homestead* (New York: Wilson Erickson, 1936; reprint, Lincoln: University of Nebraska Press, 1970); Bob Kennon, *From the Pecos to the Powder: A Cowboy's Autobiography* (Norman: University of Oklahoma Press, 1965); Mary Leefe Laurence, *Daughter of the Regiment: Memories of a Childhood in the Frontier Army, 1878–1898*, ed. Thomas T. Smith (Lincoln: University of Nebraska Press, 1996); Willie Newbury Lewis, *Tapadero: The Making of a Cowboy* (Austin: University of Texas Press, 1972); George E. MacGinitie, *The Not So Gay Nineties: An Account of Childhood in Lynch, Nebraska, As It Was Eighty Years Ago* (author, 1972); Charley O'Kieffe, *Western Story: The Recollections of Charley O'Kieffe, 1884–1898* (Lincoln: University of Nebraska Press, 1960); Lettie Little Pabst, *Kansas Heritage* (New York: Vantage Press, 1976); and Marian Russell, *Land of Enchantment: Memoirs of Marian Russell Along the Santa Fe Trail as Dictated to Mrs. Hal Russell*, ed. Garnet M. Brayer (Evanston, Ill.: Branding Iron Press, 1954; reprint, Albuquerque: University of New Mexico Press, 1981).

To these were added works by Willa Cather, Mari Sandoz, Laura Ingalls Wilder, O. E. Rölvaag, and Hamlin Garland, which blend autobiography and fiction. Not cited elsewhere but of interest are Ernest Venable Sutton, *A Life Worth Living* (Pasadena, Calif.: Trail's End, 1948), an account of growing up in the Dakotas; and Oscar Micheaux's *The Conquest: The Story of a Negro Pioneer* (1913; reprint, Lincoln: University of Nebraska Press, 1994) and *The Homesteader* (1917; reprint, Lincoln: University of Nebraska Press, 1994), both of which are semi-autobiographical accounts of life in South Dakota in the early 1900s. This variety of authors wrote from firsthand experience and observation, and while it might be argued that their writings were shaded by personal responses to events, people and place, that is basically true of all primary material consulted for this or other publications. Experience shapes viewpoint, which explains the contradictory impressions often left by a single writer or one story.

As noted in the Introduction, childhood experiences in the West have been treated largely within the subject of women's history. Among publications not cited elsewhere are Susan Armitage and Elizabeth Jameson, eds., *The Women's West* (Norman: University of Oklahoma Press, 1987); Anne B. Butler and Ona Siporin, *Uncommon Common Women: Ordinary Lives of the West* (Logan: Utah State University Press, 1996); Dee Garceau, *The Important Things of Life: Women, Work, and Family in Sweetwater County, Wyoming, 1880–1929* (Lincoln: University of Nebraska Press, 1997); Katherine Harris, *Long Vistas: Women and Families on Colorado Homesteads* (Niwot: University Press of Colorado, 1993); Julie Roy Jeffrey, *Frontier Women: The Trans-Mississippi West, 1840–1880* (New York: Hill and Wang, 1979); and Sandra L. Myres, *Westering Women and the Frontier Experience, 1800–1915* (Albuquerque: University of New Mexico Press, 1982). These lead to the obvious point that childhood is bound to the roles of women and the history of family. Here the following are of interest but by no means inclusive of available material: Carl N. Degler, *At Odds: Women and Family in America from the Revolution to the Present* (New York: Oxford University Press, 1980); Steven Mintz and Susan Kellogg, *Domestic Revolutions: A Social History of American Family Life* (New York: Free Press, 1988); Elizabeth Pleck, *Domestic Tyranny: The Making of Social Policy against Family Violence from Colonial Times to the Present* (New York: Oxford University Press, 1987); and Tamara Hareven, "The History of the Family and the Complexity of Social Change," *American Historical Review* 96 (February 1991), 95–124.

Volumes devoted specifically to children in the West are cited in the Introduction, but more prevalent in the study of children and childhood in American society are publications related to social and educational movements and urban life. Among those consulted were Daniel Beek-man, *The Mechanical Baby: A Popular History of the Theory and Practice of Child Raising* (Westport, Conn.: Laurence Hill & Co., 1977); Robert H. Bremner, *The Public Good: Philanthropy and Welfare in the Civil War Era* (New York: Alfred A. Knopf, 1980); Joseph M. Hawes and N. Ray Hiner, eds., *American Childhood: A Research Guide and Historical Handbook* (Westport, Conn.: Greenwood Press, 1985); Samuel H. Preston and Michael R. Haines, *Fatal Years: Child Mortality in Late Nineteenth-Century America* (Princeton: Princeton University Press, 1991); Elliott West and Paula Petrik, eds., *Small Worlds: Children and Adolescents in America, 1850–1950* (Lawrence: University Press of Kansas, 1992); Bernard Wishy, *The Child and the Republic* (Philadelphia: University of Pennsylvania Press, 1968); Nancy Schrom Dye and Daniel Blake Smith, "Mother Love and Infant Death, 1750–1920," *Journal of American History* 73 (September 1986), 329–353; Mary W. M. Hargreaves, "Rural Education on the Northern Plains Frontier," *Journal of the West* 18 (October 1979), 25–32; and Kathleen W. Jones, "Sentiment and Science: The Late Nineteenth Century Pediatrician as Mother's Advisor," *Journal of Social History* 17 (Spring 1983), 79–96.

An important adjunct to examining childhood experiences was the subject of place. Response and adaptation to the plains environment were integral to settlement and the development that followed, and a number of sources have dealt with the questions of psychological response, cultural identity, and agrarian idealism. More than one publication credited to James R. Shortridge is cited in the notes, but one good example is "The Expectations of Others: Struggles Toward a Sense of Place in the Northern Plains," in *Many Wests: Place, Culture and Regional Identity*, edited by David M. Wrobel and Michael C. Steiner (Lawrence: University Press of Kansas, 1997). Also of interest are Brian Blouet and Frederick Luebke, eds., *The Great Plains: Environment and Culture* (Lincoln: University of Nebraska Press, 1979); David Emmons, *Garden in the Grasslands: Boomer Literature of the Central Great Plains* (Lincoln: University of Nebraska Press, 1971); and James M. Marshall, *Land Fever: Dispossession and the Frontier Myth* (Lexington: University Press of Kentucky, 1986). Certainly Robert G. Athearn's *The Mythic West in Twentieth-Century America*

(Lawrence: University Press of Kansas, 1986) is among the books that remind us that the idea of the West still resonates in the American psyche.

The study of children in the West is intricately woven into the history
of childhood, family, women's roles, and Western expansion. It is not limited to American-born Caucasians but represents the multiplicity of ethnic and racial groups that made the plains their home. Sources cited here
and in the notes (I make no claim to exhausting *every* available volume,
article, or collection) demonstrate the great variety of contexts in which
the history of Western children may be addressed. Collectively, materials
offer an extensive resource for further study and powerful testimony to
the experiences of Western children.

Index

A NOTE ON THE AUTHOR

Marilyn Irvin Holt was born in southern Illinois, where her parents still maintain a farm. She studied at Eastern Illinois University and the University of Illinois in Springfield, and is a former editor for the Illinois State Historical Library and a former director of publications for the Kansas State Historical Society. She has written widely on the history of the American West, including *Indian Orphanages*; *Linoleum, Better Babies and the Modern Farm Woman*; and *The Orphan Trains*. She lives in Abilene, Kansas.